TAKE A G
LOOK AR(

TAKE A GOOD LOOK AROUND

JAMES C. WOFFORD

Hamilton Books
A member of
The Rowman & Littlefield Publishing Group
Lanham • Boulder • New York • Toronto • Plymouth, UK

Other books by James C. Wofford are:

Training the Three-Day Event Horse and Rider
Publisher: Doubleday 1995
ISBN 0-385-42520-1

Gymnastics: Systematic Training of the Jumping Horse
Publisher: Compass Press 2001
ISBN 1-900-667-21-5

Copyright © 2007 James C. Wofford

Hamilton Books
4501 Forbes Boulevard
Suite 200
Lanham, Maryland 20706
Hamilton Books, Acquisitions Department (301)-459-3366

Estover Road
Plymouth PL6 7PY
United Kingdom

Library of Congress Control Number: 2006935862
ISBN-13: 978-07618-3657-5 (paperback: alk. paper)
ISBN-10: 0-7618-3657-8 (paperback: alk. paper)

Design & Production: A Good Thing, Inc.

The paper used in this publication meets the minimum requirements of
American National Standard for Information Sciences—Permanence of Paper
for Printed Library Materials, ANSI Z39.48–1984

PREFACE

Those who receive an occasional e-mail from Jimmy Wofford have learned to look forward eagerly to them. You can't always guess what they are going to be about, but you can be sure they'll be unlike any others that you get. As with this book (whose content they embody) they have a very distinctive voice, always interesting, usually funny in a very original way, often provocative and occasionally poignant.

Many of the chapters in this book concern horses, reflecting Jimmy's distinguished career and wide travels as a sought-after coach and TV commentator. Others chapters (perhaps to the surprise of those who know him only as an Olympic medal-winning Event rider) are drawn from other areas of his wide spectrum of interests, from hunting and fishing to military history and even poetry. To top it all off, there is a generous sprinkling of seriously funny stories, skillfully related.

All in all, *Take a Good Look Around* is a fine example of pure 100-proof unadulterated Wofford. Pick out a comfortable chair, turn to Chapter One, and enjoy a visit with a genuine American original.

William Steinkraus
Chairman Emeritus
U.S. Equestrian Team

FOREWARD

Put this book back on the shelf if you thought it was another one of my books about training horses. It is about horses, but it is also about people, and Labradors, and trout, and quail, and ducks, and places I have been, and our interaction with the natural world. I hope you found this book filed under "humor." Given that I think almost everything is funny, you need to bring your sense of humor along when you read it. If you are unusually sensitive, politically correct, or even a liberal, you can be assured that there is something in here that will annoy you. Sorry about that; you were warned.

Over the course of an unusual lifetime, I have maintained a sort-of diary. This book is a result of that diary, and of the experiences that I describe in it. Some of the stuff in this book is pretty hair-raising in one way or another. All I can say is that for the most part, it really happened. Plus, my attitude is that if it did not really happen the way I tell it, it should have. I'm not testifying under oath here. Remember the guy who worked in the Clinton White House who testified that he had lied to his diary? Think of it that way.

The title of this book is derived from an expression in use around my neighborhood here in Upperville. When one of my rowdy friends gets over-cocktailed, his wife will typically drag him out of the party by his ear, telling him, "Take a good look around, big boy!" Meaning that he most likely won't be invited back, so he should remember it as it was at the time. I have always been aware that we might not see something, or experience something for a second time, hence the title.

Some of the chapters deal with horses, to be sure, because my whole life has been dedicated to their training and welfare. However, I have tucked those chapters a little later on in the scheme of things. Some of the chapters are funny, and some of them are sad, but that is just life its own self. The first chapters are about places I go when I am not training horses and things I do when I get there. Later on I will slip back to the horse world, with my weblogs from various Olympic and World Championships around the world. Finally, I will throw in a couple of poems for those of you who are interested to see just how badly the English language can be tortured and yet survive.

There are a couple of chapters that need a little introduction, and I have inserted some narrative where I think you might need a bit of scene setting. Any book is the result of more than one person's effort, and this book is no different. Once again Sharon Anthony has suffered through the dreaded "rough draft" process, and the results here reflect her keenly intelligent attention. Merrilyn Blue has applied her considerable computer skills to rescue my laptop from the brink of disaster more than once, and I am truly grateful.

I owe a great debt of thanks to Cathy Laws of Primedia, and Jo Whitehouse of the United States Eventing Association (USEA), who both believed, long before I did, that I could write something that people would actually want to read.

The graceful pen-and-ink sketches that open each chapter are by Jane Gaston. Her ability to capture the personality of animals and the true feel of the natural world is uncanny, and her work is an enormous addition to this book. Open the pages carefully, lest one of the creatures displayed herein leap out and sit in your lap, glowing with character.

My lifelong friend, idol, mentor, and editor, Bill Steinkraus, has been putting up with me in prose and in person for longer than either one of us want to recall right now. If you find this book readable, thank him, not me. Usually, the author takes responsibility for any and all errors. However, since this is mostly a work of humor, you might wonder, "Are they errors, or did it really happen that way?" I will leave it to you to judge.

CONTENTS

TAKE A GOOD
LOOK AROUND

PART I

HOOKS AND BULLETS

DON'T MESS WITH TEXAS

It's not the visiting new places that gets you. It's the traveling from here to there. You can start out in the best mood you have ever been in your life, but by the time that imbecile behind the airline counter gets done with you, you will be sending off vibes that would make a rabid pit bull with piles cross the street to avoid you. And if you are traveling with a shotgun? You fit the profile, buddy, turn around, drop your drawers, and bend over...this is going to hurt you more than it does me. I started to take a bad case of umbrage, but I heard two of the guys behind the counter whispering about tranquilizer darts, so I settled down, got through the experience, and headed on my way.

It had all started out so innocently:

"Warfurd, whyncha come on down ta Texas and shoot some birds?"

That was Big Al Martin talking. Now, when Big Al talks, most people listen...he didn't get that nickname by accident. I was at loose ends at the Devon Horse Show one night about a quarter century ago, and saw this 7X beaver Stetson sorta floating above the crowd in the bar.

I had noticed the hat's owner earlier in the day when he was introduced as a new director at the spring meeting of the board of directors of the American Horse Show Association. He did not exactly fit the paradigm for new directors. At that time the AHSA was a white-bread East Coast outfit, and I could tell right away that if I stuck around, there would be a culture clash of some significance. I didn't know the half of it. Anyway, where was I? Oh, yeah, in the bar. So, I walked up and offered to buy the new guy a beer, and we've been friends ever since. We have remarked from time to time about that night. I mean, it is a hell of a thing when the bar at a horse show sponsored by Anheuser-Busch runs out of beer.

So I headed down to southeast Texas to shoot birds. I love Texas. I couldn't live there, but I love it. That is one tough country. Everything down there either has teeth, a stinger, or thorns. We were shooting on Al's lease on the Santa Fe Ranch, about 35 miles south of Falfurrias, which is the darndest collection of prickly pear, catclaw, mesquite, and scrub oak you ever saw. This part of the world is so tough, there is a species of snake, called blue indigo that lives on rattlesnakes. They go looking for rattlers, provoke them into striking, and then grab them by the heads, crush their skulls, and eat them. (I know you don't believe me, and I really don't give a bleep. After you look it up, you can apologize.)

Most of that stuff you have heard about Texas is true. First of all, it is hard to understand distance down there. The family that owns the Santa Fe Ranch owns over 800,000 acres in the area. Any bigger, and you could fit the state of Rhode Island inside it. I think the immense distances account for the unusual nature of the people who live there. If your personality did not expand to help fill up all that space, you would wind up feeling pretty small. This also helps explain a Texan's subtle conception of the truth. It is not as if there are going to be a lot of witnesses, and if that's not the way it happened, well hell, that's the way it ought to have happened.

Robert Heinlein said, "An armed society is a polite society." Texans are real polite. They call waitresses "Ma'am," they watch their language in front of ladies, and they take their hats off when they are introduced to a member of the fairer sex. If a cowboy says he will do something, he'll do it. You don't need a written contract. If he said he'll do it, he'll do it. You have to meet a few cowboys before you start to understand cowboy pride, but that concept is alive and well down there. It is antiquated, but charming, and it suits me.

Things in Texas are pretty democratic. The old geezers at the next table may be some down at the heels cowboys, or they might own so many cattle that they have lost count. Either way, you could spend the whole meal with them and never know. One of them went to the Wharton School of Business and the other one spent the blizzard of '57 in a line cabin teaching himself to read with a King James Bible and the collected works of Shakespeare. You could go broke betting which is which.

Meals in Texas are a serious endeavor, all three of them. Bird shooting at this time of year starts out early, since the bird dogs can't run for long in the heat, and it usually gets really hot by 10 a.m., unless it gets cold, in which case it gets really cold. This means breakfast is served about 5:30, and I'm not talking about raisin bran either, or any of that other fancified health food stuff. I mean eggs, potatoes, sausage, flapjacks, toast, flour tortillas, enough coffee to float the *Queen Mary*, and the ubiquitous salsa piquante. Border food would be lost without this staple. Just as you need a long-handled spoon to sup with the devil, you need a long-handled spoon and a healthy dose of suspicion before you tuck into any of this salsa wholesale. It is a part of every meal down there and runs the gamut from a mild red tomatilla sauce that, in judicious quantities, even the likes of me can enjoy, to a green concoction that could double as paint remover.

The local's taste buds have long since taken a permanent vacation, and a searing dose of this stuff will produce a grunt of approval and a gruff accolade: "Tasty." If you were smoking a five-dollar cigar after you had a dose of it, you could blow smoke rings from both ends at once. Still, just because you were able to handle it at breakfast, you had better check it again before lunch. Each little café prides itself on its salsa and make it up fresh throughout the day. This means that if Mamacita is in a bad mood, or gets distracted, the lethality of the potion can vary from serving to serving. And that all takes place at breakfast.

Lunch, or "dinner" in Texas, is another serious piece of work. Cowboys will drive 30 miles each way, for a good chicken fried steak and a slab of pecan pie. Chicken fried steak is an art form in Texas, like haggis in Scotland. It hangs over either side of a 12 inch platter, has been pounded into some semblance of tender, been breaded and deep-fat fried, is slathered in white gravy that can clog an artery at 50 paces, and comes with freedom fries to complete the picture. And don't forget the hot sauce...a cowboy would go into withdrawal without that salsa. By the time one of these fellahs gets done with this item, a toy poodle would starve to death on the leavings. Meals like this are the reason that God invented siestas.

After driving 30 miles back to the dog wagon and a nap that is closer to a coma than a little shut-eye, the party heads back out for the afternoon shoot. Al had arranged with Dale Elrod to organize the shooting and bring some dogs. Dale and I go back a ways and I always look forward to seeing him. Of course, it takes a while to see him. When Dale wanders over to make his howdies, he blocks out the sun. Big Al might have it over him for girth, but Dale is hell for large. You take a deep breath before you shake hands with Dale, 'cause you are not sure you are going to get your hand back anytime soon. It is like putting your hand in a vise press. But then he smiles, and you feel like you have come home again.

I'll tell you a story about Dale in a minute, but you need to meet the other two members of the group. Adrian Gubert spent a portion of his youth jumping out of perfectly good airplanes into strange and exotic locales, so that he could shoot people. I tell him that it is obvious that the shock of all those landings has shaken all his brains out his other end. About all that is left is an inalterable habit of not doing anything he doesn't want to do with this spare time that the Lord decided to give to him, a "screw you" streak a mile wide, a driving desire to see good dogs work quail right, and a pair of eyes that twinkle with the intelligence that he does his best to disguise.

Then there's Butch. I have met Butch a couple of times, but I never can catch his last name. And Butch doesn't give a damn if I know it or not. He has made his living training cow horses and quail dogs for over 60 years now. He has gone from eager to elder statesman, and then on to the condition he is in these days, which can be summarized as "Hell, I'm going to drive the wagon for these piss-ants and see how bad they can screw it up this time."

The wagon is Adrian's. A Kawasaki Mule, with all the quail shooting doodads, it is built for a couple of humans, with eight bird dogs in the cages under the seats in back. So when the five of us get off this thing, we look like clowns getting out of a car in the circus. Add to it that we are heavily armed, and usually in a sweating hurry and you have a pretty serious promenade. If you watched this group show up and unload, bristling with loaded shotguns, you wouldn't know whether to laugh or to hit the deck. There is an elaborate choreography to getting off this machine when one of the dogs goes on point. First of all, Butch positions us behind the dogs, cuts the fire out of the Mule, rolls his toothpick from one side of his mouth to the other, and gets this faraway, sardonic look on his face, like "you think these boys screwed up that last covey? You ain't seen nothin' yet!"

Dale heads towards the dogs, either crooning or "Whoa!"-ing depending on the situation. Al is left-handed so he heads for the right side of the covey, while Adrian and I just head where the other guy isn't. I can miss them just the same from the middle or the outside, and Adrian doesn't miss, so it doesn't matter. All of this is taking place at a fast walk, because these birds are not going to hang around waiting until you get your karma squared away. So we walk up, the covey (and they are all big coveys this week, 20–25 birds) flys somewhere we did not think they would go, I shoot twice, swear, and then go help Al and Adrian pick up their birds.

By now Dale is watching his dogs, who are about half a county away, making bird on the singles. If the dogs are young, or untrustworthy, Dale begins to mutter blood-curdling imprecations involving capital punishment or worse. This is nothing but an act. For all his size and strength, Dale is astonishingly gentle with his animals, and they respond to it. It takes a little longer for him to make a dog, but when he is through, that dog will find birds, hold them down until you can get there, track the cripples, and fetch the downed birds to hand in fine style. Watching someone with fingers the size of a New Braunfels bratwurst picking thorns out of Mollie's pads is a sight you won't soon forget.

After one or two tries at the single birds, we walk back to the Mule, accept our constructive criticism from Butch, load up, and head up into the wind to look for another covey. Things were pretty good the two days I was down. We moved 14 coveys the first day, in a howling wind, and 18 the second day. We had to walk over a good part of southeast Texas, but it was worth it.

Speaking of walking, cowboys know how to walk. I don't mean the physical act of covering a sizeable distance by putting one in front of the other; I mean the style and idiosyncrasy of each cowboy's gait. No ghetto gang banger can get close for having a stylish walk. John Wayne's walk was OK, but there was not quite enough pain in it. The old guys down here have a hobbling, wincing, slightly round-shouldered pace. Imagine they are lame in both legs at once, and you'll start to get the picture. If you filled their boots with carpet tacks you might improve it a little, but not much. But the thing you need to understand is that they don't limp. A cowboy would sooner die than limp. If you limp, it means you feel pain, and of course a cowboy is supposed to be beyond that sort of thing. Limping is for sissies, or even worse, Democrats. A cowboy's walk is in the same category as the ribbon a soldier wears on his chest. Their descriptions of the occasion are laconic.

"Nah, I was bulldoggin' an' had a steer flip on me down at the PRCA Semis in Uvalde a while back, an' put his horn through my lung."

"And the next thang I know, that durned horse is going straight over backwards."

Their walk is a reminder of past dangers and accidents, of work done well in spite of pain and hardship, of struggles won and lost with creatures weighing 10 times as much as the cowboy...well, not Big Al, but that's different.

Quite simply, old cowboys walk like this because they are physical wrecks. Someone once asked a cowboy why the cattle and horse business was not more mechanized. "Cause you can't find a machine to take the abuse a cowboy can" was the reply. It is funny to watch the young cowboys walk, because they all have the same bowlegged, hobbling pace as their elders, even though they don't hurt yet. Hell, nothing hurts when you are that age. No, the reason they walk like that is because they are practicing. If you fool with horses and cattle long enough, you are going to walk funny, and that's all there is to it. Limp? Never. But a little hobbling? Well, that's just life its own self.

One of the best things about Texas is that a lot of the stuff that happens you don't even need to lie about. The truth is good enough. Plus, you don't want to start that lying stuff, 'cause the first liar never wins anyway, at least not around here.

I mentioned earlier that I was going to tell a story about Dale, and I don't want to forget. Actually, I won't ever forget...I still wake up in the middle of the night sometimes, getting ready to pull the trigger!

What happened was this: About 1990, Dale, Big Al, and I were shooting on the King Ranch, in the La Presa pasture, east of US 77 around Kingsville. We had been having a pretty good day, plus in that company, it doesn't matter if you shoot a bird anyway, because you are having so much fun. We were hunting Dale's best dog, Blacktop, and cruising a caliche road. A covey flushed loose up ahead of us, flew over a wire net fence by some stock pens, and settled down into the sacahuista grass. This was like found money to us, so we pulled up, hopped out, and headed for the spot where we had seen them go in.

When we got to the fence, Al said, "I'm not going to climb that fence for a couple of birds, ya'll go ahead."

This is cowboy talk for "my knees are killing me, 'cause I didn't listen to the doctor, and kept on bull-dogging even after I blew both of them out."

By this time Blacktop was on point at the edge of the sacahuista. Dale and I did not need any more encouragement, so we climbed the fence and walked into what we thought was some birds, with Dale about 10 feet to my left.

I realize now that Blacktop had his head cocked kinda funny, but I had seen the birds go in there, and I thought I knew what I was doing. Quicker than I can say it, a full grown wild boar burst out of the tall grass, spotted Dale, lowered his head, and charged him. This was not a good thing. This hog probably weighed 175 pounds, he thought we had him cornered, and he had a bad attitude about it. Hogs look slow, but when they want to, they can move like lightening for a short distance. So when he burst out of that grass with a full head of steam, it didn't take him long to arrive. Feral hogs develop a set of tusks on them that are as sharp as any razor, and with one swing of their head they can lay your leg open from your ankle to a lot higher. Cowboys don't normally mess with hogs that are in a bad mood.

Now right away a couple of things happened that were good things. First of all, I didn't shoot. I had my father's 12-gauge Browning over-and-under, loaded with # 8s, but the hog was too close to Dale for me to shoot. The next good thing that happened was that as the hog ran at Dale, Dale jumped straight up in the air, and tucked his knees. About the same time, Blacktop decided that he was going to join the fun, so he grabbed that hog in the back end, and started to chew his way up to the front. Blacktop made contact just in time to interrupt the hog's swipe at Dale. I reckoned that was a good thing, too.

So the hog ran at Dale, Dale jumped up, Blacktop grabbed him in the ass, and as the hog passed under Dale, he threw his head up, caught Dale's boot with his tusk, and spun him like a top. I was watching this show with some interest, and I guarantee you that Dale was four feet off the ground, he spun one and a half times around his belt buckle when that hog hit him, and he landed flat on his back. Considering Dale's size, it was probably about a five on the Richter scale. Now, did I mention the prickly pear?

Mucho prickly pear. God invented prickly pear to improve mankind's profanity, and so far it is working. Also, did I mention the noise? Let's take a moment to consider the metaphysical aspects of sound and time. The first thing I noticed about this situation was that time slowed down until everything seemed to be moving in slow motion. I had time to see the bristles on that hog's snout as he came by the first time...oh, yeah, that hog wasn't done with us yet...I could see the slobber coming out of Blacktop's mouth, as he improved his grip, and I could see the prickly pear spines, sticking out of Dale's leg. I mentioned the prickly pear, didn't I?

When Dale landed on his back he did not just land on a flap of prickly pear, he did not just get a bunch of prickly pear spines stuck in his leg, he landed dead solid perfect in the middle of the goddamnedest patch of prickly pear you have ever seen. Top to bottom, Dale's backside was covered up in prickly pear spines. Naturally, the force of impact broke off every one of those spines, so Dale's discomfort meter hit the peg at this point.

The next thing I noticed, along with time slowing down, was that the noise level had improved considerably. The instant Blacktop saw that hog, he started growling like all the demons of hell, that hog naturally started squalling pretty vigorously about the hole Blacktop was gnawing in his ass, and what else? Oh, yeah, Dale. Well Dale was in a mess, and his attitude was going south by the second. Every time he moved, he drove those prickly pear spines deeper into his backside, so he didn't want to move. But, he knew that hog was around someplace because he could damn sure hear him, so he had to move. Sort of your classic rock-and-a-hard-place dilemma.

Along about now, Dale was mixing his futile attempts at extricating himself from the prickly pear with urgent, stentorian commands to me along the line of, "Shoot that son-of-a-bitch! Shoot him!" Between Dale coaching me in the finer points of hog shooting, Blacktop growling and gnawing, and that hog complaining to high heaven, I had quite a symphony going.

By now, the hog was past us, and headed for Port Aransas. "So far, so good," I thought. "Nobody is dead yet, and that hog is leaving town. Maybe this will have a happy ending after all." Well, that's when the situation started to really deteriorate. Blacktop dropped his grip on the hog to take a deep breath, at which point the hog switched directions, and headed back for the deep grass that he called home, with Blacktop growling and gaining. They passed in front of me, and the dog was far enough back for me to shoot the hog in the face. I knew I couldn't kill him at that range with # 8s, but I didn't think I would be helping his eyesight any, if I could hit him in the face. Anyway, I hit him in the face; he flinched and squalled, and continued his progress. So much for plan A.

Blacktop figured out that the chord of a circle is shorter than the circumference, caught up with his old playmate, and latched on again. This had the unhappy effect of dragging the hog around in a clockwise circle, with Blacktop celebrating and braggin', and that hog bitchin' and moaning. Locked up in this manner, they made a full circle in front of me. Somewhat dismayed at my first shot's lack of effect on that hog, I reloaded while I waited for another chance. Naturally, Dale's imprecations were growing in volume and urgency, but his message was basically unchanged: "Shoot him! Shoot that son-of-a-bitch!" Considering that Dale, Blacktop, and that hog could have been covered with a horse blanket, I thought this was one of those good ideas whose time had not yet come.

I don't think the right phrase is, "As luck would have it...," it's more like, "Uh oh, it's my turn." The hog made a sharp high-speed turn, which flung Blacktop off into the tall grass, and left the hog facing towards the last man standing...me. By now Dale was getting to his hands and knees, and the symphony was continuing. If anything, it was reaching a crescendo, but of course the three participants had had some practice.

I remember thinking that while I needed to let the hog get closer this time, that wasn't really going to be a problem, as that hog was headed right for me at a high rate of speed. I had two shots left, which was another one of those good things, as my first attempt about six months ago had made him shrug and grunt but did not slow him down any to speak of. He was about 10 yards away when I shot and I got the same shrug and grunt routine as the first time, so I waited another year and a half and took my last shot.

It is a well known fact that the Lord takes care of drunkards, fools, and little children. I guess He figured me being a three-time loser and all, He would step in and make sure that last shot went where it needed to go. I saw a red gash open up just in front of his right shoulder, and heard the shot column as it hit him. That hog was graveyard dead before he hit the ground, and I could have touched his nose with the barrel of my gun without moving my feet...that's how close he was.

Time started to act a little more normal in my neck of the woods, and I looked over at Big Al, who had hung over the wire fence throughout the entire performance. He was a little ways off, but I could see his shoulders shaking, and he was laughing so hard he had to wipe tears from his eyes. We pulled prickly pear out of Dale's backside for half an hour, but I wasn't much good at it, as about 10 minutes after I got back to the truck my hands started to shake so badly I couldn't hold my Leatherman to pull on the stickers.

"An adventure like that could drive a man to drink," I said.

"There's some beer in the cooler," Dale said.

"How long were we out there?" I asked Big Al.

"About 30 seconds," he replied.

"Seemed like a lifetime," I muttered.

And that's how Dale and I got to be good friends, and why to this day we both swear that Blacktop was the mostest bird dog we ever saw.

DUCKIN'
THE BAYOU

You are kidding yourself if you go duck hunting to shoot ducks, at least these days. There aren't many ducks around anymore, and the way I shoot, they are safe with me. You go to see how it comes out. Any time you mix men, loaded guns, mud, various types of complicated machinery, birds, fish, water, Labrador retrievers, and booze, you get a bunch of unpredictable outcomes. About the only thing for sure is that you don't know what's next...that's why you go.

What happened was that my good friend, Tim Dudley, called me and said for me to schedule a trip to Bayou du Pont, south of New Orleans. I had to think about it, for a nanosecond. "OK," I said. So away we went. Tim and I have been friends since the early seventies, which covers a lot of territory and a fair amount of whiskey. If he says we need a road trip, I'm ready.

Now Bayou du Pont is not your romantic, Faulknerian, Spanish-moss-in-a-mangrove-swamp kind of bayou. This is an enormous grass marsh about an hour south of New Orleans, slap in the middle of a gas and oil area, with all the attendant odors, sights, and sounds. And flat? If you stand up on the bow of a mud boat, you can see all the way to Galveston. The living accommodations are not what you would call romantic either. Comfortable, yes. Romantic, no. The cabin is basically two double wide trailers, bolted together and placed on a one-acre man-made oyster shell island Throw in a cook shack of similar size and design, a metal-roofed shed for the duck boats and pirogues, and another shed for the diesel generator that drones away 24/7 and that's the outfit. The area can hold ducks in astonishing numbers and variety, and when things are right, you can shoot a limit before the guides can get the boat stowed away.

You drive south from the New Orleans airport for about an hour, to the little village of Lafitte, La....As in Jean Lafitte, the pirate. His descendants still populate the community, with the same tribal customs and loyalties. They have an unyielding determination to live close to nature, and far from any taint of the law or its minions. Cajuns speak a soft, wonderful, melodious patois which, if you listen carefully, sounds almost like English. Well, it is and it isn't. "Water" becomes "wah-tah," "New Orleans" becomes "Nawlin's," and "Louisiana" becomes "Loo-siana." They switch between English and French with an unconscious ease, except when they have been drinking. Then they lapse into some other dialect, unknown to the sober. Take it from me, if you can understand a Cajun when he has had a snoot full, it is time for you to quit!

These people are throwbacks to an earlier time. They have the closest correlation between want and need of any substrata of society in the western hemisphere, and are a strange mixture of restless energy and astonishing sloth. They will sleep on their porch for several days in a row, immune to all spousal importuning, then wake up at some ungodly hour and pole a pirogue for miles in a howling gale at the prospect of shooting ducks.

They think nothing of working several 30-hour shifts on a shrimp boat interspersed with short naps, collecting their share in cash at the dock, blowing it all on a day or two of Bacchanalian debauchery, and then showing up at the boat, flat broke and ready to ship out again.

A Cajun is born with a GPS in his head. I swear that one of them could navigate across the state of Louisiana blind-folded in a whiskey induced fog. I guess you never get lost if you always know where you are.

I have a good ear for dialogue, but I cannot reproduce much of it here, because it is usually so obscene and profane that even a Democrat would blush. Combine this with the limited topics deemed suitable for polite society, and I am nearly at a loss to describe the scene. Anything to do with prevarication, flatulation, fornication, procrastination, or intoxication is fair game. Likewise included are illegal activities such as intentional violation of various game laws, dynamiting fish, misprision of various felonies, or unlawful sexual congress with the neighbor's wife when he is away on the shrimp boat. Don't forget gluttony, cupidity, or stupidity. Basically, these guys think the Lord handed down 10 Recommendations.

Natural humorists, their conversation is replete with clever turns of phrase, interspersed with a casual and appalling profanity and obscenity, and flavored with a matter-of-fact acceptance of things as they are in the world.

The Chinaman probably leads this parade. He is not Chinese, he just has a slightly oriental cast to his features. In other circumstances they might be sinister, but in this context they are merely comical. First of all, the Chinaman is big. Not tall, not fat, just big. If you told him to haul ass, he would have to make several trips. Yesterday, Big Curtis came around the corner of the canal, and found the Chinaman perched on the side of his boat, naked from the waist down. "Wad you be doin,'" Curtis inquired. "Man, ah had to fart," replied the Chinaman," but ah fahgot to check it first an' ah done shit mah drawers."

Well, don' be trowin' dem in de bayou," said Curtis, "you be mak' ah fish kill!"

"Be too late for dat," said the Chinaman, pulling up his now underwearless camouflage trousers.

Given a couple of stiff snake tonics, the Chinaman is a stream of consciousness that would put any comedian to shame. Speaking of the casual disregard for the niceties of property rights as practiced by some of the denizens of Lafitte, he recounted the following: "So, ah look don in de wah-tah between the boat an de whaf, an' ah seed de bahdy. An' we pull him out wit' dah boat hook an' ah say, 'dat be LeReaux, and he gad sum nasty cuts on hisself! An' he be daid, beside!'

"An' Junior say, 'yeah, an' he don' be stealin' no mo', neda.' " You never know where the humor will arise, or why, but it will be there. Little Curtis was napping on the couch in the cook shack when a discussion ensued about a party in Lafitte that night. Lil' Curt declined, on the basis that it would "jus' be family fightin'." Presumably, this meant no knives or blunt instruments, and was thus beneath his notice. "You don' be need to worry 'bout dat, neda, you don' be invited," Lil' Curt was told. "How cum dat?" Lil' Curt asked. "Cause you gad too many teefe an' not nuf tat-toos," was the reply.

The first morning, Ralph and I had a little nip of peach brandy on the landing before debarking, just to salute the first glimmerings of another glorious day at Bayou du Pont. Well, one thing led to another, and my experienced Cajun guide, born in the marsh, a GPS in his head, raised under the shadow of the North Star, and all that...got drunked up and drove our mud boat slap into an island in the middle of the marsh at full throttle. "I'da just as soon ducked this part of the bayou," I remarked to Ralphie, when he pulled himself out of the pile of duck decoys he had landed in. It took some labor by both of us, plus Curtis's 125 pound Labrador Mule to extricate the boat, as the only thing left in the water was the propeller. When curious bystanders sought an explanation, Ralph replied "Ohhhh, dat peach brandy...she sneak UP on you!"

Duck hunting doesn't always provide nonstop action. You can sit there for hours and days with nothing happening. The only advantage is that you never know where the conversation will lead. Out of nowhere, I asked Ralphie the difference between a coon-ass, and a cajun. "Dat be simple" said Ralphie,"uh Cajun be uh coon-ass wid' webfeet."

Later in the week, Ralph and I were sitting glumly in a blind, wondering if we were ever going to shoot a duck, when a fusillade of shots broke out in the neighboring marsh. "Think some ducks went in over there?" I enquired. "Nooo, dat be somebody shootin' de man wha' ask 'im duck huntin'," replied Ralphie.

I figured that was my clue to pack my bags and head for Upperville.

A GRAND TIME ON THE GRAND CANAL

THE DUNRAVEN ARMS

The Irish are no stranger to hyperbole. Americans, on the other hand, tend more towards understatement. When an American says "the Grand Canyon," you had better brace yourself. Rushing majestic rivers, cowboy chic colors that defy any palette, and if you fall off the edge? You might die of old age before you hit the bottom. So when my Irish ghillie told me we were going to catch a trout in the Grand Canal, we weren't on the same wavelength.

My wife Gail and I had decided to come to Ireland for a few days to rest up before a more strenuous part of our journey. It is not every day you get to combine a visit to watch the Ascot Gold Cup with a long-awaited tour of the battlefields of Normandy Beach, but that was the plan. Thus Ireland, and a stay at the

Dunraven Arms, seemed like a good idea. It has been 15 years since I have been here, and things have changed.

Landing at Shannon Airport, I got the first of many surprises. The countryside was in the grip of the worst heat wave in nearly half a century. Now when an Irishman gets a chance at some vitamin D, he doesn't mess around. There is more pasty white flesh on display than you would find at a Brittney Spears concert. No one in Ireland has ever heard of melanoma, and you can forget about sunscreen, because they don't worry about all that. Anybody without second-degree sunburn has either just finished 30 days of detox, or is out on early work release. Just let it out and parboil it, that's the ticket.

Anyway, the thought of a couple of days without an organized activity was too much for me, so I naturally turned my thoughts to fishing. I had never caught a trout in Ireland, and I was badly feeling the lack of it. A quick call to my new best friend, James Robinson, set the arrangements, and away we went. Ireland is a different country than the idyllic, poverty-stricken, peaceful backwater I remember. Nowadays, business gurus refer to Ireland's economy as the "Celtic tiger." The combination of low tax rates and membership in the European Union has made an incredible impact on life here, and as Louis Murphy says, "The country is awash with money." The Irish themselves are just as I left them...charming, vital, full of life, and with their subtle conception of the truth intact. Any fisherman can tell you that there is a time and a place for expansive versions of the absolute truth, so I figured I would fit right in with an Irish fishing guide...after all, you are looking at someone who has kissed the Blarney Stone three times, so far. You can usually tell right away if you and your guide are going to get along. Thus it was with my Irish version of Isaac Walton. By the time we had gone five minutes down the road, James and I were contentedly slanging politicians of every stripe and persuasion.

James is a ruddy-faced man, wreathed in a cloud of cheap cigar smoke, and content to hide in a nearly impenetrable brogue. An engineer by training, he did not set out to become a guide. Like most people who are overtaken by a passion, it just sort of happened. One thing led to another, and now he guides full time, while his wife runs the sporting travel agency that has sprung up in tandem with his guiding activities. Our destination lay on the other side of the town of Limerick, and it was obvious that Ireland has improved, if your definition of improvement is more money, more cars, more motorways, and a McDonalds on every corner.

But I said things had changed? Yesterday, when we arrived at the Dunraven Arms, Louis turned us over to a handsome young gentleman of obvious Pakistani or Indian descent. "Mick will be showing you to your rooms, sure an' he will," said Louis. "Na den sorr, if ya'll be after followin' me," said Mick. I barely managed to conceal my surprise at this son-of-Erin brogue emitting from the mouth of someone not obviously of Celtic descent, and delivered our bags into his care, to good effect. I told you Ireland had a lot of surprises, and the influx of immigrants has left its stamp on Ireland. But it is a fair bargain, because Ireland is leaving its stamp on them as well.

"The river is too low and warm entirely to be holding any fish ahttall," James, proclaimed, so we would catch a trout or two in the Grand Canal instead. You can imagine the expression on my face when we pulled up to a seemingly lifeless ditch.

Originally built in the 1800s to carry Guinness beer from Dublin to Limerick, it is now a combination of a walking path, a public right-of-way, and some serious trout fishing. At first glance, the water appears still and lifeless, but like so many things Celtic, there is more going on under the surface than one might imagine. The current here is relentless, as subtle as you could ever hope to imagine, and if your presentation has any flaw in it, you are out of luck. The trout here get a fair amount of pressure, and the stupid ones are already in the frying pan. Tying on a Daddy Longlegs seemed like a good idea, and I was rewarded by two strikes in my first two casts. The canal holds an astonishing number of brown trout, and I was gleefully employed for a while, walking gradually up the bank and catching fish. The fish here must be feeding on some of that Guinness that spilled out of the barges, as they are fat and opinionated.

Nothing good lasts forever, and the water finally warmed up to such a degree that the fish decided that a siesta would be the right thing to do. "You can work away if ya like," James said, "but ya'l only be torturin' yersel' ta no avail." I can take a hint, so we packed our rods, and continued the journey towards Normandy Beach and beyond. It bothers me that there are so many places I haven't seen yet, and trout I haven't cast to yet, and curiosity bumps I haven't scratched yet, so I needed a change of scenery anyway. By the way, if you are having as much fun as I am, don't tell anyone, or Congress will outlaw it.

ALASKA? JUST BEARLY!

I was raised on stories about Alaska, so I have always wanted to see it in its natural state. Since mankind can't leave well enough alone, I've been thinking that I'd better get up there pretty quick, before we mess it up. September is a pretty month in that part of the world, and the fishing is supposed to be the best. Besides, Gary Johnson had invited me up to the lodge that he runs in Good News Bay.

For those of you who don't know Gary, he is one of the best guides in the world, and a good friend besides. Quite a few years ago, I was fishing on the Snake River, near Jackson, Wyoming, and ran into Gary. You never know when you are going to meet a new friend. Gary is one of those people that you might not see for six months or a year at a stretch, but when you meet up again, it is as if no time has expired since your last meeting. You are just friends, that's all.

Now, the first thing you notice about Alaska is that you really have to want to go there. It is a long way from anywhere, even with a layover in Anchorage.

When you step off the plane in Anchorage, there are two bears mounted in glass cases on either side of the concourse. One is the world record polar bear, and the other one is the state record grizzly bear. Both are imposing specimens, to say the least.

"Hope that's as close as I get to one of those suckers," I muttered to myself as I walked past them. Little did I know.

Driving from the airport, named for Senator Ted Stevens, to my motel for the night, I passed by the world's largest float plane lake, named surprisingly enough for Senator Ted Stevens. Hundreds of float planes sit there quietly, testifying to the effect of distance on life in the Arctic. If there are no roads, you either fly or float. End of story.

Senators have been compared to members of the board of directors for the whole country, but they are more like the ancient pharaohs, building monuments to themselves. Ever driven through West Virginia? Then you've seen what I mean...If it moves, Senator Byrd wants to tax it, and if it doesn't, then he wants the U.S. tax payer to paint it and hang his name on it. Of course, I am an equal opportunity insulter. Stevens is a Republican, and Byrd is a Democrat, but they are both professional politicians, which says it all.

My motel room window looked west over Cook Sound. It was a strange sensation to think that Siberia is only a few hundred miles across the Bering Sea from here.

A brief taxi ride on Saturday morning took me to the air charter service that was supposedly flying me to Good News Bay. The plane looked like a flying shoebox and had to be 40 years old. Now, the good part is that it had to be tough to last this long, but the bad part is this might be the trip to end all trips, if you catch my drift. Anyway, I had choices...I could turn around and never see all those lovely fish (not happening), or I could take the last tramp steamer into Good News Bay (but it would not get me there before the first snowfall.) I figured I hadn't cheated death for a year or more, and I was in the mood for fish, so I stepped on board.

After an hour or so, I was wondering if I had made the right decision. One moment we would be thousands of feet above flat, trackless tundra, and the next we would be threading our way between glacier-covered mountains, precipitously rising and falling as the updrafts and downdrafts tossed us around.

"You wanted an adventure," I thought to my self, "now quitcher bitchin!"

An interminable time later saw us making the turn into Good News Bay Municipal Airport. The locals proudly brag that the average commute to work in Good News Bay is four minutes. What they forget to tell you is that the only industry around here is fishing for dinner, or taking a boat across the Bay to whack a caribou for the freezer. A metropolis Good News Bay is not. A half mile dirt runway, some small huts made out of any scrap material that was handy at the time, a combination post office-general store, and that is Good News Bay.

We met Gary and the other guides at the plane, and transferred our considerable plunder to the shore, where I had my first introduction to those inventions of the devil called "jet boats." They call them jet boats because they are propelled by a jet of water, and they make you feel like you are in a jet plane, as they can reach speeds up to 35 miles an hour. They only draw a couple of inches of water, so you can go whizzing across gravel bars with dry rocks showing on either side. Add to this their maneuverability, along with the winding nature of the Good News River, and you have all the hair-raising experiences you need for one day.

"Don't look down," was Gary's advice.

Fifteen minutes later, or a lifetime, your choice, we arrived at the camp. The lodge is not exactly roughing it in the Alaskan outback. They have permanent walled tents, a drying room for wet waders and raincoats, flush toilets, and wonder of wonders, showers with plenty of hot water. I took all this in, but my attention was drawn to the river. Every minute or so, a sleek, silver shape would break the surface, and disappear again, always tending upstream. My feverish enquiries were met with the laconic reply that the silver salmon were passing through on their way to their spawning grounds 60 or so miles upriver.

"Yup, a big push of silvers is coming through right now."

I hurriedly rigged my rod, grabbed a couple of likely looking flies (any color you want, as long as it is pink) and asked the manager where it was OK to fish.

Pointing upstream, Mike said, "Just walk up along the bank, and fish anywhere for as long as you want. Be back for dinner at seven."

Now those are the sort of instructions I can understand, so I grabbed my vest and various fishing toys and headed up river. Other members of the party had been gripped with the same fever, and were already standing along the bank near the camp, and hooking salmon. I hadn't come to Alaska for the social aspect of it, so I kept walking along the bank until the rest of the party had been left behind. I finally turned a corner, and could look all the way up the Good News River valley, to Subdulik and Barnum Mountains in the far distance, and beyond.

"Not another person in sight, and all of Alaska ahead of me," I thought, "Life is good."

I caught the first salmon of my life that afternoon, and more. I don't remember exactly how many. You either catch a bunch, a few, or you get skunked. It doesn't really matter, anyway. What matters is that for a little while you are alone and completely a part of nature. I think that is why I want to fish in running water.

When you step into a river, you are stepping into the veins and arteries of the natural world, and you become a part of it, and when you have a fish on your line, the line whispers to you of where that fish has been and where it is going, and for an instant you are a part of all of that as well. And the water moves at the speed it is supposed to move, and things slow down for you, and for that moment you feel as if you are where you are supposed to be.

Unfortunately, I was supposed to be at dinner by seven, so I reluctantly reeled in, and headed back down the bank to the camp. I was not in a hurry to get there for several reasons. I hated to leave all those fish. It felt vaguely sinful to leave a river teeming with fish while there was still daylight enough to see them. Plus, I was not looking forward to meeting a bunch of strangers that I would have to be nice to, and make polite conversation with.

"Ah, what the hell," I thought, "I've had double hernia surgery. How tough can this be?"

So I stopped by my tent, poured a triple shot of all-purpose brown, and headed up to the mess hall. The first thing I thought when I wandered in was, "Where did all the geezers come from?"

It took me a second to figure out that if you are young enough to be able to enjoy Alaska to the fullest, you are too young to be making enough money to be able to pay your way up here. This is a spendy kind of trip, by my measurements.

So, most of the guests up here tend to be of a certain age. They all turned out to be nice people, which is the usual rule, and most of them keen fishermen and—women. Where I was raised, asking personal questions was considered a bit rude. Because of my travels, and the career that choose me, I have gotten accustomed to being interrogated. However, I still find it a bit off-putting, and I make a game of it, to see how long I can go without answering that dreaded question,

"So, Jim, what exactly is it that you do?

My answer to this is usually something vague, along the lines that I teach riding lessons. Then the fun begins, 'cause either way I'm sunk. One type of person will get a funny look on their face, like they just smelled a dead mouse. You can see them thinking, "Oh, oh, saddle tramp!" and they say "How nice." Then they drop me like a bad habit. That is fine with me, as that was the desired result in the first place.

The second response is the one I dread, because it usually goes like this: "Say, why didn't you say so? You know, my daughter rides, and just last weekend she..."

Well, you get the drift. The down side of the second result is that I have to stick around for a while, but the up side is that I can just smile, and nod approvingly from time to time. Proud papa will carry the conversational ball for me. If you have enough scotch, you can stand most anything.

Based on my conversational experiences at the mess hall that night, there are three things you will never hear in a fishing camp:

"I just love the way my fly line is the same color as the wrapping on my fishing rod."

"Would you like some more of this Chardonnay?"

"Do you think these waders make my hips look big?"

Anyway, much to my surprise, I survived my first dinner, and came outside to see that there was plenty of light, and fish still rising as they worked their way upstream. "Sleep when you get home," I thought to myself, and grabbed my rod.

I staggered back down the path to my cabin several hours and innumerable salmon later and bumped into Gary, who asked me how I was doing. "Fished myself to a standstill," I mumbled. I could tell from the twinkle in his eye that Gary understood the nature of my compulsion, and approved. Turning back down the path, Gary reminded me to set my alarm, so as to be on time for the fishing in the morning.

"He has got to be kidding." I thought, "There is no way I would sleep through a trip like this!"

There had been a lot of talk about grizzly bears at dinner, so my subconscious must have been tuned in to grizzly bears. Sometime during the night, I got up to take my kidneys for a walk. The generators that provide power for the camp had long since been turned off, and I did not want to go to the trouble of lighting the propane lantern, so I just stepped out onto the deck.

Standing there in a night lit only by stars, I suddenly sensed a dark shape, and watched as a bear crossed the river a few yards upstream from the camp and disappeared around the corner. It was too dark for me to discern any details, so I could only watch a black shape moving with a sense of power that gave me pause, and made me glad I was removed from his path. I stood there for a moment, savoring the experience. It suddenly occurred to me how strange it is to be someplace where it is totally dark.

You might think you live in the country, but it is rare to find total darkness anymore. I was up during the middle of the night at home not long ago, and there was more ambient light around than you could shake a stick at...blue power lights from the computer, yellow lights from the microwave, orange lights from the blinking clock numerals on the VCR. (One of these days, I'm going to figure out how to set the clock on that damned thing.) Anyway, you might think you live somewhere that is dark, but you don't know the half of it. Go to Alaska in the dark of the moon—that's dark.

I've spent most of my life getting up early and getting dressed in the dark. Gail thinks it is because I am being thoughtful and not waking her up. That is certainly part of it, but little does she know that I am afraid to look at myself in the mirror that early while I shave. I mean, there is just so much the human body can stand. Of course, that look was nothing to the look on my face a few hours later when Gary knocked on my door and announced that I was literally about to miss the boat. Yup, slept in on my first morning in Alaska.

"He burst into a flurry of activity" does not begin to describe my condition. Five minutes later I was standing on the dock, puffing and sweating, and ready for the adventure.

Gary introduced me to George Guidry, my fishing partner for the day, and we headed downstream. Things were a bit slow, so I asked Gary to step into the river next to me, take my rod, and show me how to catch a salmon. (For the uninitiated, this is a surefire way to get things on the river moving after a dry spell.) Guides hate this, as they invariably hook the largest fish of the day, which can enrage some clients.

You can guess the next part, as Gary immediately hooked a real race horse of a fish. That made me laugh, but it was nothing to the paroxysm I went into when the handle on my Hardy reel suddenly rapped Gary smartly across the knuckles ninety-eleven times in quick succession, while a male silver salmon made the most of his opportunity. Take a stick and whack a watermelon as hard and as fast as you can, and you will get a close approximation of the sound of that reel handle doing the wild thing on Gary's hand.

"Oh, yeah, I forgot to tell you...my reel is broken" I mentioned.

""Now you tell me," Gary muttered ruefully, as he licked the blood off his knuckles.

"Serves you right," I pointed out, on the basis that no good deed goes unpunished. "I thought the dudes were supposed to catch all the fish."

"Here, now you try," Gary said, and gleefully handed the rod and defective reel back to me.

I've forgotten the fish, but I'll never forget that noise. You don't travel because you know what is going to happen. You travel to see what happens next.

George wandered back to see what the ruckus was, discerned the cause, smiled vaguely, and wandered back downstream in search of the perfect cast and the perfect fish, which as any true fish-a-holic will tell you, is always the next one.

After dinner, I thought that I would go back to the gravel bar where I had fished the night before, and catch one or two more fish. Salmon were taking my fly on a fairly regular basis, so I was naturally absorbed in my dream world-privacy, running water, and abundant fish. "The only thing missing is a little nightcap," I thought, "I'll just catch one more, and then I promised Gary we would drink a little scotch together."

I probably shouldn't have done that.

As I led a chrome-colored salmon down to the gravel bar to release it, I suddenly heard a sound like a herd of horses, galloping along the bank towards me.

"What the...?" I thought, and looked up to see a grizzly bear come skidding to a halt on the bank just above my gravel bar. Without thinking, I threw both arms in the air, squalled "HEY!" at the top of my voice, and lit out for the other side of the river at what Gary later described as a "Jesus-walk." The bear rose up on its hind legs and peered at my rapidly departing form, 10 yards away and accelerating. Now I'm here to tell you that when this sort of thing happens to you, you can forget all that romantic stuff about "I heard the owl call my name." There is no poetic "a golden glow seemed to surround the bear, who had now become 'BEAR, the uber-bear,' the symbol of all power, of all life and death, the very archetype of all bears, and all power, and all life and all death and..." You know the sort of thing.

Let me tell you what really happens when you are convinced—not worried, not concerned, but *convinced*—that you are about to be eaten by something a lot farther up the food chain than you are—what happens is that you are the repository of millions of your caveman ancestors' successful primal bear experience. The ones who ran survived. The ones who didn't run got taken out of the gene pool. Buried deep in your DNA is an anti-bear gene, and when a bear enters your world, that gene takes over. And the message that gene delivers is..."*run*, and don't stop running until the bear gives up, or catches you, whichever comes first!"

So, you run. It doesn't matter that you are running through waist-deep water over slick rocks. These are nonessential details compared to the fact that you are too frightened to look over your shoulder to compare your progress with that of the bear. You don't slip on the rocks, your ankle doesn't hurt, and you are not out of breath. (That comes later.) I had not looked back yet, being grimly intent on reaching the far shore. Several fellow fishermen, including Gary, had come running up the shore to see what the noise was about.

"If I can just reach the shore," I thought, "I won't have to out-run that bear anymore, I just have to find one of those guys who is slower than I am, and out run him!"

As I reached the assembled group, I could tell from their expressions that I could finally hazard a look back. The bear, followed by a smaller companion, had decided that I was more trouble than I was worth and turned away. At this point, Gary burst into laughter.

"What's so funny?"

"You must have really wanted that fish," Gary said, and pointed behind me. It was only then that I realized that in my panic I had hauled a 12-pound salmon left-handed across 50 yards of river. Gary later said I was making a bow wave, and the fish was skipping behind me like a flat rock on a farm pond.

"Come on, my man," Gary said and slapped my back, "you look like you could use a drink."

"I don't think one is gonna do it," I muttered and headed for the bar.

I usually know what time and which day it is. I woke up about daybreak the next day, and had to look in my datebook to figure out what day it was. That doesn't happen to me very often. I'm going to turn 60 in a few months, and I have been thinking about time a lot lately. I suppose a close encounter of the bear kind lends a certain emphasis to stuff like this. I know I'm getting older; I am just a little tentative about it. I've never been old before, so I am not exactly sure how to do it. Your prostate gets bigger, and your brain gets smaller, for sure. Otherwise it is OK, so far. Practice will make perfect, I guess.

It did not help that on my way to breakfast I passed the two young Eskimo ladies, Samantha and Jessica, who do the work around the camp. Probably named after soap opera stars. I startled them slightly when I spoke, and they both turned sharply to see who it was. I had the eerie sensation that both of them went through their reproductive checklist in a flash and decided I wasn't of any interest. Male? Check. Anglo? Bad sign. Geezer? No way.

"Good morning," I said. "Good morning, Sir," they replied, all chocolate eyes and pheromones, and giggled. I guess giggling is hormonal and gender related, not a product of culture, ethnicity, or environment. I passed them by and went into the mess hall feeling slightly depressed. Being called "sir" by 16-year-old girls serves to confirm one's suspicions about the progress of time.

The presence of a stack of flapjacks and scrambled eggs restored my humor, and made me think about life in a fishing camp in the back end of nowhere in Alaska. I guess the closest analogy would be living on the moon. Nothing that you are using except the water is produced here. Imagine the path a light bulb has to take to give you light in your tent in the morning, and the expense involved. A $25,000 jet boat can be grounded by the lack of a 25-cent part, if you don't have a spare. If you drop the camp's only five-eighth-inch wrench in the river, it can be a couple of weeks before you finish that repair job. People who live in the wilderness tend to be careful and sparing of the things they use. They know what it will take to replace anything out here.

George, Gary, and I headed upriver, and my mood improved out of all recognition. I saw a perfect analogy for the ecosystem up here late this afternoon. A coho salmon had completed its spawning run, drifted back downstream, and died. Its remains were submerged in about a foot of water, and a school of salmon fry were happily nibbling on the bits of flesh that were gradually flaking loose from the carcass. That was the cycle of life up here, in a nutshell. Meeting a bear, and realizing you are not at the top of the food chain, makes you more aware of all this.

Gary told me a story about a river system closer to Anchorage, where people have been going fishing and elk hunting for a long time now. About 10 years ago, the salmon got overfished, and their numbers declined dramatically. Almost immediately, the health of the elk suffered, and the size of their antlers was noticeably reduced. Yet, as the salmon, now protected, rejuvenated the system, the elk recovered as well. Biologists deduced that salmon were bringing trace minerals in from the Pacific that did not exist in the river system, minerals that were essential to the health and development of the elk. The death of the salmon each year was necessary for the life of the elk.

Mother Nature is a complicated old lady, and we don't always understand her as well as we would like to think we do. There is a synchronicity to life everywhere; we just need to learn how to look for it, and accept it.

I awoke the next morning to a soft, soaking rain. This raised the level of the river enough to give us access to the Middle Fork of the Good News, and George, Gary, and I spent a companionable four hours along a gravel bar below Lookout Mountain, catching salmon and solving the problems of the world. We went back to the camp for some hot soup at lunch, and the Sirens of the Pillow captured George.

Gary and I resisted their importuning and fished for rainbow trout in the North Fork, but to no avail. Still, a good day in soft rain and grey fog. I am back in my tent as I write this, with my laptop perched on my knees. The rain is tapping quietly on the canvas roof, and scotch never tasted better. The generator was turned off a while ago, which means the regular lights don't work; so the propane lantern is hissing away, spreading a slightly yellowish glow. Bonnie Raitt and Jose Menendez are singing "Quando llega la noche" in the background. I could get used to this.

So, the next morning, things got better. "George is part owner of the operation here, and he has to stay back and do some work," Gary said, "so it's just you and me this morning. What do you want to do?"

"Let's get in the boat and just keep going until we run out of river," I replied. So that's what we did. Of course, there is more to it then that. First of all, you have to understand that turning Gary and me loose to go fishing is like two Jack Russell terriers touching noses, and departing for parts unknown. You don't know exactly what is going to happen, but you do know it is going to be unscripted, the participants are going to be gone for a long time, and they are going to return in a disheveled condition. Next, about Gary's boat. Gary doesn't see quite as well as he used to, so he recently franged his boat pretty good on a gravel bar, and if you don't keep the balance (aka, the "trim") just right, the boat will cavitate (aka "vibrate like all hell"). What this boils down to is that with only two of us in the boat, we have to put a lot more weight in the bow, which is where yours truly comes in. We are going to run this jet boat wide open for an hour, which means if we don't want to cover 20 miles of bad road, we need to get the trim right.

My good friend Bill Steinkraus is notoriously more learned and erudite than I am, so at this point he would probably start drawing parallels between my pose and Joseph Turner, who in the

1840s hung his head out of a train during a rainstorm. Turner did this so as to experience what he was about to capture on canvas. Billy really does think like this. Of course, he has a distressing habit of shooting spoonbills, too, but I've about got him broke of that habit. Nobody's perfect.

I tend to be a more linear thinker, so the image that sprang to my mind was a Labrador retriever, leaning forward into the wind, with his ears flapping. That was me, up on the bow of this jet-propelled water rocket.

After a few minutes, my confidence increased, and I started to ignore Gary's advice about not looking down. We were passing over schools of salmon heading upriver for their spawning grounds. We were going so fast that I could not distinguish individual fish, merely silver and red streaks as we flashed over them. At times there were so many red male salmon in a row that they all blended into a blood red streak, and I had the sensation that we were suspended above a river of blood.

Which, in a way, we were. Everything along the river system depends on the salmon returning each year. They are the lifeblood of the tundra. If they don't come back, the hawks and eagles, the bears and fox will not store up enough fat to survive the winters up here. No salmon, no life in the tundra.

I've been here for several days now, so I am an expert on Alaska, and I finally get it. Up here, it is all about sex. You are born here, grow up and get strong, travel, come home, have sex, and die. Kind of reminds me of a few of my younger fishing buddies, come to think of it. The way those guys are going at things, they must be expecting an early demise, but at least they will die happy.

Happy doesn't begin to describe it when we ran aground about an hour later. We were in the valley between Barnum and Subdulik Mountains, at the mouth of Barnum Creek. There had only been one fishing party there in the last month, so we thought there was a pretty good chance of catching some rainbows, Dolly Varden, and grayling. We hiked up the creek for about a mile, and Gary soon put me onto my first Alaskan rainbow. Let me tell you, these are a different kettle of fish. They hit like a sledge hammer, jump like a kangaroo, and pull like a locomotive. Pound for pound, they fight harder than the salmon I have caught so far. When you bring them to hand, they are brilliantly colored, with scarlet stripes and black pepper corn spots.

I had just returned my first ever Alaskan rainbow to the water when I heard those three little words you never, ever, want to hear your Alaskan guide say:

"What was that?"

"Huh?" I responded.

"Listen," said Gary, and sure enough, I could hear something very large meandering through a slough just on the other side of the willows that framed the creek.

"Might be an elk," Gary offered.

"Might not," I suggested.

"There's that. We're downwind, too," Gary responded. "Let's mosey on down this creek a ways, and see what happens."

So what happened is that two trout fishing maniacs "moseyed" past a quarter mile of the sweetest looking trout water in all of Alaska, with never a backward glance, if you can call "moseying" looking like a pair of heel-and-toe racers heading for the finish line in the Olympics. Anyway, no harm, no foul, I always say.

"Did you find out if it was a bear?" you might ask.

"No, and we were not sticking around long enough to find out, either."

"Gary, you are usually pretty good about having everything we might need out here, but you messed up this time." I said.

Now Gary takes his guiding seriously. Everything is squared away when you go out with him. So a statement like this gets his attention.

"Like what?" he asked.

"Next time we come up here, bring more claymores."

Gary spent a sizeable portion of his youth as a self-professed expert on the placement and usage of claymore antipersonnel mines, so he saw the logic of my argument immediately.

"We can do that. Now, let's go catch you a Dolly Varden." This suited me, as I had never caught one of them, and was badly feeling the lack in my fishing resume.

There is something about the Fishing Gods that the more you want some thing to happen, the less likely they are to let it happen. Thus it was with Dollies. We fished back down Barnum Creek, but no luck. I was a little ahead of Gary, when I heard him say, "Fish on."

If I can't catch one, I can darn sure get a picture of one, I thought. So I stuck my rod under my arm, started looking for my camera in my vest, and waded towards the bank. As I got to the shore I suddenly realized that I had my camera, but not my rod. Somewhere on the way to the bank I had dropped my rod in the river, and it had been swept downstream.

In a situation like this, your heart doesn't just sink; it plummets. The problem is not the replacement cost of your favorite rod and reel gone missing in the wilds of the Alaskan wilderness. Nor is it the inconvenience of not having anything to fish with in the middle of a fisherman's paradise. The problem is the loss of a tangible connection with the places you have been, and the things you have done.

You can buy another rod and reel, and you can borrow an extra rod from your guide. What you can't do is replace the scrape that you put on your new rod, fighting the first fish you ever caught with it, at the Rolling Rock Club in PA. A new reel won't have the gouge from that boulder on the Gold Medal section of the Rio Grande down in the Sangre de Christo's, where you slipped, bent the **** out of your reel, and pounded it back into shape with a rock. It is not about the material things themselves. It is about the things you have done with them, and the experiences you have had, and the things you have learned through them along the way.

When I throw my father's Browning to my shoulder, I am doing more than bringing up a shotgun to shoot at a bird. I am bringing up my father's memory. You can't replace memories, so you are reluctant to lose the tangible reminder of something that otherwise is only a will-of-the-wisp in your mind.

You can see why I was more than a little upset at the thought of my favorite Winston 5-weight, and favorite Hardy reel, bouncing along the bottom of the creek on a slow journey to the Bering Sea. I looked up- and downstream for it, and was in the process of giving up, when the Fishing Gods relented, and my rod floated to the surface almost under my feet.

"Look's like my luck has turned," I thought, and resumed my quest for a Dolly Varden, which by now was assuming mythical status. "Try this," Gary said, and handed me a different fly. Bingo!

Dollies are not very big in this section of the creek, but they make up for size with enthusiasm. So it was a couple of minutes before I was able to bring my first Dollie to the bank.

"Let's get a picture," said one of the world's most experienced fishing guides, and proceeded to squirt that fish up into the air like a grapefruit seed. Dollie landed on the bank at our feet, and started a dance that would put St. Vitas to shame. I was going to say "a dance that would put Michael Jackson to shame," but "shame" and "Michael Jackson" don't seem to fit in the same sentence, do they? This fish disco did not do Gary's temperament any good. He had been quietly seething for the past half an hour- at his inability to get me hooked up with this mysterious new species.

Now Dollies are notoriously slimy, and Gary's lunges at the fish only succeeded in coating his hands with slime, and rendering the fish even more elusive. The situation was not helped by my uncontrollable laughter. I had given up on the camera by this time, and was alternately doubling over and wiping my eyes.

All this motion was messing with Gary's outfit pretty badly...his hat had come down into his eyes, his rod was tangled in my line, and the sling on his Remington 870 had slipped, and was starting to strangle him. His next grab at Dollie was followed by another escape. Not to be out maneuvered, Gary delivered a heel stomp to this fish that would have warmed the heart of any martial arts instructor. The only problem was that the fish was already back in the creek and leaving for parts unknown.

"Uh, I think she gave us the slip," I ventured.

"I don't want to talk about it," Gary muttered. "Let's see if we can catch another one."

When I did indeed catch another one a few minutes later, I had learned from my recent experiences.

"Here," said Gary, "let me get a picture of it for you."

"That's OK," I said hastily, "I've got it." And I did, too. I drug that hussy far enough up the bank that she couldn't escape, got my camera ready, and snapped a shot in between wiggles. So that photo of a Dollie in my photo album is of my second Dollie...the first one is the one that got away.

Never ones to miss an experience, we decided to float farther down the river, and see if I could land a silver salmon on my five weight. The answer is yes, but it is in the same category as shooting an elephant with a .22 rifle. After you do it, you say to yourself, "What the heck was I thinking?"

Robert Ruark always said, "Use enough gun." "Yeah" I would agree, "and use enough rod, too."

"I've had about as much fun as the human body can stand," I told Gary, so we lit out for the camp. After dinner, Gary said, "What do you want to do tomorrow?"

"Let's point it up a different branch of the river and go until we hit gravel," I replied.

"Sounds like a plan," Gary said.

The next morning that's what we did, except that we hit a grass bank; but you get my point. We had made it all the way above Tiviaguk Creek on the south fork of the Good News when we came to a sharp bend in the river. This used to be known as the "Hole-in-the-wall" but is now known as "Gary's Corner." Hitting a grass bank at 20 miles per hour is nature's way of telling you that you have gone as far upstream as you are going to get today, and you might as well get out and start fishing, so that's what George Guidry and I did. And what fishing! We caught rainbows all the way back down, mostly on sculpin patterns.

No one had been able to get this far up river since June, due to low water conditions, so the fish were not exactly spooky. I added to my photo album today, and noticed the foliage has been turning. I was startled by the speed of the change between the first of the week and now. But it is OK. September is early fall in Alaska, so that is what is supposed to happen.

The fishing being desultory, I took a nap at one point. Things were pretty comfortable until I rolled over, and noticed a fresh bear paw print in the sand next to my head. It was not just the proximity of the foot print, although that was disconcerting enough, but I could stand with my wading boot inside this print and have room left over on both ends. I hastily pulled myself up, and glanced around, wild eyed.

"Haven't seen one that big around here for quite a while," Gary remarked. "Wonder how the fishing is downstream a ways."

"Let's go see," I said, and elbowed him aside on my way down the river. One thing you learn in Alaska is to know your place in the food chain.

A trip like this is not really about the fish. They are the excuse, but the real reason is the new sights and smells and sounds you will notice, the ecosystem you will step into, and the things you will remember. Still, you need to take note of your fish on a day like this, if only because it isn't often given to you to land a wild rainbow nearly a yard long, with no one else within a half a mile of you, while an eagle circles over your head, and water that has never felt a human rushes by your legs.

As I released him back into the river, I stood back up and looked north up the valley, and thought, "OK. I'm ready to go." And I meant it in both senses of the word.

I mentioned earlier that I had been thinking about life and death a lot lately. My sixtieth birthday is just around the corner, and my body is starting to warn me that nothing is forever. That has made me sad, and I've been feeling pretty low. But it seemed like when I put that fish back into the river, that I realized that I was going to slip back into the river myself pretty soon, and that is the way it is, and that is the way it ought to be. It seems like when I let that fish go, I let go of myself, too.

I had another day of fishing to go, and Gary would run the boat onto a rock this time, and we would catch some more fish, and stay up late the last night, and finish the last of my scotch. We would brag about the silver salmon we caught on a dry fly, and muse about the quality of the fishing, and the beauty and abundance of Alaska. But I was ready to go.

The blood-red fish are mostly gone now, far up river, taking care of business, and insuring that there will be a next generation. Their blood has somehow transferred into the leaves, where it will soon fall to the ground, so as to be ready when spring comes to the valley, and the next generation of salmon heads down-stream, to see what life is about.

Gary dropped me off at the airport, and we said the gruff, awkward goodbyes of men who care for each other.

"Let's do it again," Gary said.

"Next year," I replied

And I will, too. I want to come back and get in the boat, and go as far upriver as any human ever has, and then fish my way back down to civilization.

But in the meantime, when people ask me if I have ever been to Alaska, I smile, and say "Alaska? Just bearly!"

BALOUSH ON
THE BITCHES

I should have known it was going to end ugly. I rolled out of my bed early, in a good mood, with nothing new hurting. The weather was perfect for trout fishing, and I had an unscheduled day off. My tea was the perfect temperature, the cereal was crisp, the sun was shining, the light on the Blue Ridge was exquisite...life was good.

Today was Election Day, so I drove over to the polls on my way out of town, to do my small part in keeping those bloodsucking, tax-raising liberals beat back. You know about this recent move to "get God back in politics"? Well, I am all for it. I figure if the politicians are praying, I can see their hands, which means they can't be trying to get them into my pockets at the same time!

Where was I? Oh, yeah, my good day was continuing. There was no line at the polls, so I could be on my way to the trout stream in no time. Plus, my good friend Carter Eskew, the notorious liberal, was just coming in at the same time. Do you have any idea of the warm, fuzzy feeling that came over me, at the thought that I got there just in time to cancel his vote with mine? I guess the Big Trout Guide in the Sky was sending me a special moment, knowing what he had in store for me later on. With my civic duty done, and well done, if I do say so myself, I headed north on I-81 for the Yellow Breeches (aka "the bitches"), in PA.

The traffic was light, the weather was glorious, and Nacho, my Labrador, had his usual fulminations and gaseous eruptions under control. I mean, I was having such a perfect day that the local convenience store in Boiling Spring even had a copy of this morning's *Washington Times*, for Chris' sake! I never thought it wouldn't last.

Probably my first mistake was stopping in at the fly shop. "Well, been a little tough lately, but you might try this, and this, and this, and this, and that'll be $34.00, my friend." A small frisson of doubt crept into my mind, quickly banished by, "Naaahhh, hell, I caught fish here before...no big deal."

So I pulled down to the upper parking lot. "What the...?" I muttered. Cars everywhere. "Of course," I suddenly realized, "I'm not the only trout genius who noticed that today is a good day to go fishing." Somewhat distracted, I had to swerve to avoid running over a guy in waders. "Now what?" was quickly followed by "Uh oh!" This guy and two others like him were kneeling on prayer rugs in the parking lot, facing upstream, and mumbling imprecations to the Fishing Gods. Now I was really spooked.

But I figured, "Hell, how tough can it be?" So I suited up, little knowing how tough it could be. As I walked down to the stream, one guy passed me on his way out. Sobbing uncontrollably, he was being supported by two buddies, who were patting his shoulders and making "there-there" noises. Walking to the bridge, I saw another guy standing on the bridge. He raised an eight foot, six inch Thomas and Thomas up, broke it over his knee, tore off his fishing vest, and threw the whole kit and caboodle into the river.

He passed me screaming, "My reach cast had a microdrag, my reach cast had a microdrag!"

"I guess he's through for the day." I thought to myself.

The next part was finding a place to fish. Every 50 feet there was another fisherman, most of them geezers. After being put on hold, I got a number and stood in line, and finally stepped down into the water. Nacho waited patiently on the bank. He is a good companion, but sees no reason for getting wet unless it is in hot pursuit of a duck. The only thing he worries about is being left behind. He has had the much-needed effect of controlling my temper on the river. If I get my line hung up in the trees, I have to mutter under my breath, because if I start to yell and swear, Nacho thinks I am mad at him.

"You stay," I said to him, as I stepped into the Bitches.

"No worries, Boss," I could hear him reply, "I haven't lost anything in that cold water."

Did I tell you the Bitches is spring-fed? Well, this sucker runs cold, let me tell you. (You see where I am going with this, don't you?)

So, after all this, I began to fish. And fish. And fish. And...well, you get the picture. I started with the fly that worked last week. Nothing. The fly the fly shop guy said would work. Nothing. I tried every fly I bought today. Nothing. By now, fish, some of them of respectable proportions, were starting to rise all around where I was standing. I suddenly realized that I had been standing in the same place for nearly two hours, trying to outwit something that basically does not have a brain, just a wide place in his ganglion. Two hours of hard fishing, and nothing to show for it.

At this point, I realized I was skunked. No two ways about it. Just then, I heard a voice behind me, "Mind if I fish here?"

I turned around, and invited yet another geezer down, explaining that I had lost the feeling in my legs, due to the cold water, and that I was going to get out and walk around until I got the feeling back in them. "Any luck?" I politely inquired, as I turned for the bank.

"Nah, pretty tough," Geezer replied, "I've only caught four."

"Oh, really", I said, as casually as I could. "What were they taking?" I asked.

"A CDC Caddis," he said. "Here, I'll give you one of mine."

"Damn right" I thought, "the one and only fly I don't have with me."

As I turned towards him, my ice-numb toes caught on a root, and you guessed it, Baloush! As I surfaced, I heard him say, "Ain't that something! That's the exact same place I fell in two days ago!"

Through chattering teeth, I wished him good luck, and headed for the car. And thus it was that I was home before dark on Election Night.

NOT IN A
COON'S AGE

As it turned out, the raccoon was not rabid.

What happened was, yesterday I decided I needed to go fishing in the Shenandoah. My wife had sent me on a search-and-seizure mission to Winchester, so I thought I would kill two birds with one stone. Packed my stuff, got my list, put on my wet-wading clothes, remembered to bring dry clothes to change into, iced tea, rod, reel, extra flies, license, bug spray...good to go.

The Shenandoah is about 100 yards wide and flows north along the Blue Ridge Mountains, so the scenery is as good as the fishing. About the only cast I did *not* catch a fish on was the first cast...mostly smallmouth bass, along with a few perch, some bigger than my hand. Most of the smallies were about 10 inches long, and acrobatic as all get-out.

I stayed out there for almost two hours. There are not many nicer ways to spend a blazing hot Virginia June afternoon, than standing in a river, the water about 68 degrees, running down over my—anyway, you get the picture.

By now I had fished myself to a standstill, so I waded to the bank, and walked up to the truck to change. There was not much traffic on the dirt road, so I stepped to the off-side, opened the door, stripped down, and reached for my dry clothes.

Something behind me made a chirping noise. "I wonder what kind of bird *that* was?" I thought. More chirping. I looked around, still in full birthday suit mode. "Oh well," I thought, and reached into the truck. I felt something hairy brush my ankle, and there was more chirping. When I looked down, there was a half-grown raccoon, standing at my feet, with his head down in my wading shoe, slapping me in the leg with his tail. Let me tell you, the speed of light had *nothing* on me. I did not jump into the front seat, I levitated. And, when I got there, I commenced to cuss and squall at that goddamned raccoon for all I was worth. He looked up at me, shrugged, and went back to investigating my wading shoe, probably for the same reason my Labrador rolls in my sweat socks. Finally, I grabbed some wet clothes. Remember, there were still a lot of wet clothes around, as I had not improved my sartorial condition in the meantime. I commenced to slap the living daylights out of that raccoon. This is tough to do, when you are *standing* on the front seat of the truck but you can perform miracles if your stress level is high enough.

Rocky finally deigned to notice me, and my next over hand smash with the wet fishing shirt took him right in the chops. At this, he drew himself up, gathered his dignity, and retreated leisurely down the trail, chittering to himself as he went. I must be in pretty good physical condition for a man my age. My pulse came down to normal within 30 minutes.

The moral of the story is next time, I'm going to change in a phone booth, with the door locked.

WELL, I CHEATED DEATH AGAIN

SUNDAY, JUNE 29, 2003

Well, I cheated death twice today, and you will never guess what happened next. After a few days of teaching people to ride in western Canada, I thought I was due a respite, so I headed for the Elk River, in Fernie, BC to catch a few trout. I flew from Kamloops into Vancouver and on to Cranbrook on a vomit comet. We followed a line of thunder storms into the airport, with all the attendant turbulence and other dramas. This was no fun.

Metal tubes that leave the ground basically defy the laws of physics, and it gets a bit hair-raising when you fly through air that isn't there any more, so to speak. I am usually a good shipper, but dropping 100 feet at a time puts me off my feed. Plus, towering stratocumulus and lightening has never been my thing. Needless to say, I was fairly adrenalized by the time we touched down, even at such a late hour.

It did not help my nerves when the car rental android said I did not have a reservation. Further investigation revealed that (1) I was not in the computer, for the very sensible reason that they do not have computers in Cranbrook, and (2) it did not matter anyway. There were plenty of cars to rent, because nobody in their right mind would fly into Cranbrook under these conditions. I ignored the implied insult, grabbed the keys and headed for the parking lot.

New trick: when you are over-traveled and under-slept, and it is late, and you can't find your (expletive deleted) rental car, hit the red button on your key chain. Then figure your car is the one with the flashing headlights and honking horn. It worked for me, so I hopped in and struck off for Fernie, reportedly one hour's drive away.

The nights are short in BC, and you have to sleep quick. It was still twilight at 11 p.m. when I pulled out onto what passes for a superhighway up here. This is not the sort of area where they roll up the side walks at dark. That would mean that there were sidewalks to roll up. Next thing I know, there I am zooming down the Elk River valley with the Canadian Rockies all around me. There were still thunderstorms aplenty, on both sides of the river valley, and enough lightening in them to run my three girls' hairdryers for a week. Between being jacked up on adrenaline, driving too fast on a strange highway in a rice rocket, dealing with the shakes from my recent airborne acrobatics, and cranking the Allman Brothers up to nine on the radio, you can imagine that I was still pretty awake.

That's probably why I was able to cheat death for the second time in one day. I had passed a red Mustang just before Elko...5.0 liter engine, big tires, some serious road rot, a casual attitude towards white lines, the whole story. The driver was obviously one of those types who feel emasculated when another driver passes him, so he came on in hot pursuit...why? Well, to ask for them back, I guess. However, not even BC Bubba could find a passing lane for the next 10 minutes, so he contented himself in the meantime with some serious bumper humping.

I was getting just a little bored with his act when God, in the shape of Bambi, decided to take a part of the action. Just ahead of me, on the side of the road, I saw Bambi's eyes glisten in my headlights. I had the eerie sensation that I could see her thought processes as I came roaring down on her, with Bubba 15 feet behind me:

"Should I jump? No. Yes? No. Yes?"

Naturally, I did not wait for her final answer, but made a serious effort to push the brake pedal on that rice rocket through the floor board. No Bambi. No noises or sudden jolt. No broken glass. So far, so good.

"But, but, what about Bubba?" you might ask. Well, I am glad you asked. As I turned the next corner, I could see in my rear view mirror that he had come out of the 2X flat spin he had just survived, and was parked on my side of the road, at a standstill, facing the other way. So I did what any Good Samaritan, practicing Christian, red-blooded American boy would do. I muttered "Thank you, Jesus" and punched it.

I pulled into Fernie at oh-dark hundred, thinking I had had enough hassle for one night. You guessed it, no desk clerk. "In an emergency, call..." said the sign.

Goddamned right this is an emergency, I thought. "Not only is my not getting to bed an emergency," I said to the voice at the other end of the phone line, "it could be dangerous for your health!" Joe from security seemed to get the point, and duly arrived with the key. They knew I had a reservation because they have computers in Fernie. Suffering succotash, if I had known he weighed 300 pounds, I wouldn't have been so rude on the phone.

"Hey, Joe," I stammered, "How ya' doing?" Now this question, when asked in BC, invariably produces the same response: " Uuuunnnnhh, not sah bad. How 'bout yourself?" And so it was tonight. Joe seemed to take no notice of my formerly abrasive attitude and was content to show me to my room, and wish me a good night.

I have had enough excitement for one day. I am going to rub some all-purpose brown on the sore parts, and turn out the lights.

MONDAY, JUNE 30, 2003

Nobody had to rock my cradle last night. I did remember that I had to meet my guide at nine, so I set my alarm for an early wake-up. The thing about Canada is that it is not the U.S. Nice motel, lovely scenery, great facilities, and no one awake, so no breakfast.

But my philosophical musings were taking second place to the sensation that my stomach thought that my throat had been cut. A few minutes later, I was pulling into the little town of Fernie, BC. Fernie doesn't wake up any earlier than the village where I was staying, so no diners, no restaurants, no 7-Eleven, no 24/7, nothing. Do you know what it means to be a stranger in a strange land? Beset by a sea of troubles, perplexed by strange cultures? And starving to death as well? Then you know what I felt like when I turned the corner and saw up ahead, like a mirage, or a vision from paradise...yup, the Golden Arches. Saved.

Thus fortified, I met Russ Trand, who assured me that we were going to have the day of all days, if only the Fishing Gods would cooperate. Guides always say that when you first meet them. I don't know about you, but I always believe them. What the hell, it is polite, and it might even be true.

On our way downtown to buy a license, I happened to notice a chocolate Labrador on a street corner, with his staff. "Funny," I thought, "that looks just like Oliver, but Glynis Schultz took my clinic yesterday, three hundred miles away in Kamloops, and there is no way she would be up here in the middle of nowhere, or that I would bump into her on the streets of Fernie." May be Freud was right, that there is no such thing as a coincidence, but I am not sure where this particular point on the celestial space-time continuum fits into the Devine master plan.

Further investigation revealed that Glynis and her fiancé had driven up for the "skookum" mountain biking. The Brits and the Yanks are not the only countries separated by a common language.

Laughing and shaking our heads at strange coincidences, Russ and I drove to the landing and put forth in his brand-new drift boat. We were barely into the water when I caught a nice cutthroat trout. "Oh, yes, we are the masters," Russ and I told ourselves. But the Fishing Gods can smell hubris, and decided to punish us by sending winds of gale force. The wind blew all day long, steadily gusting from 20 to 30 miles an hour. This takes all the fun out of casting a #6 Chernobyl Ant with a 5-weight rod. By the end of the day, my arm would be so tired I had to rub my face in perplexity with my left hand.

The Elk is a beautiful fishery, but it is tough under those conditions. We did catch some fish, 15- to 20-inch cuts, fat and healthy and fantastically colored. We earned them.

What else? Oh, yes; did I tell you about cheating death for the third time in 24 hours? Due to the wind conditions, Russ passed up several good looking places to fish, on the grounds that they were lined with Cottonwood trees, which are notoriously prone to toppling over in windy conditions. We rowed cross river to avoid one such place, and thus were only deluged by the splash that a 75-foot Cottonwood tree made as it landed in the river, right behind us! I think it made a lot of noise, but I could not tell, because all I could hear was my pulse rate in my ears. Kinda makes a fellow wonder how many other bullets he has ducked by being in the wrong place at the right time, or whatever.

"A situation like that could drive a fellow to drink," I mentioned to Russ.

"Try Rip's and Richard's, just over the bridge into town," Russ replied.

Don't touch that dial; I'll be back with more from the Elk River.

TUESDAY, JULY 1, 2003

Well, I did not cheat death today, but I had fun anyway. Tuesday dawned bright and early, but I was not around to appreciate it. Sleeping in is unusual for me, but I indulged myself this time around. After a morning spent basically puttering around, I headed for the river. There is a faint path towards the river, which goes through some fairly deep woods. One old-timer in the fishing shop had told me, "Naaah, we don't get much griz' up this way any more." I forgot to ask him how much griz' was too much. You can believe I was mighty awake coming through the woods towards the river. If you happened to hear an out-of-tune, high-volume rendition of "I'm riding Old paint and I'm leading Old Dan..." that was the sound of my griz' repellent going off.

Fortunately, it worked, and I spent the afternoon walking along the bank, stepping into likely spots and occasionally catching 12- to 14-inch cutthroats. I prefer this sort of fishing to drift boats. The boats move at a relatively high rate of speed, and you spend your day popping short casts into pockets of calm water, picking your line up before it snags a branch, and repeating the process. Walking upstream, one has time to scan the water ahead, make a plan, and then swear mightily when you screw up your back-cast. Much more fun. Plus, I have become one of those fishermen that John Gierach speaks of, who becomes "addicted to solitude." Anyway, I tried golf when I was younger, but it was too easy and I got bored.

Did I have a good day? All I can tell you is that it was 5:45 p.m. before I noticed that I had not set my watch correctly, as there is no June 31. Remember Satchel Paige? "How old would you be, if you didn't know how old you was?" That's the frame of mind I was in. I leave here tomorrow, bound for Bozeman, Montana, for a fishing trip with my partner in crime, Jim Wolf. I will spend three days there with him...if that does not provide me with new material for my weblog, nothing will.

WEDNESDAY, JULY 2, 2003

Wednesday was not my favorite day of the week, this week. Travel is a disconcerting experience at the best of times. When you throw in badly organized international border crossings, stress increases on an exponential basis. I don't mean to say the line to get back into the U.S. was long, but the lady in front of me had her passport expire while we waited.

By the time I got to Bozeman, I was ready for a drink and an eight-hour nap, so naturally my ride did not appear. Half an hour later, just as I was reaching for my cell phone to give someone a piece of what remained of my mind, what did I see appear at the curb? A Suburban of indiscriminate color and uncertain vintage, festooned with old flies and new rods, and containing my fishing buddy, Jim Wolf, and our guide for the next three days, Pete Howell. They piled out of the 'burb in a cloud of beer fumes and excuses. They were both grinning like a skunk eating chocolate, and babbling about the wonderful day they had just had on the Gallatin River. I managed to control my exuberance.

Some negotiations then ensued...dinner was proposed at a fern bar in Livingston?...nope, not interested...but, they have really good steaks?...I ate in Denver...the best looking waitresses in the Rockies?...whatever...a list of fine scotch whiskies two pages long?...NOW you're talking!

Thus it was that it was late when I arrived at the Yellowstone River Lodge, outside Livingston, Montana. Our room is 100 feet above the Yellowstone River, and the rushing sound of the river is a pretty good soporific. I think I am going to like it here.

THURSDAY, JULY 3, 2003

On Thursday, we were up and at 'em, as Pete had told us that we were bound for Sixteen Mile Creek, a spring creek of some repute. I finally figured out that the name is derived from the fact that it is sixteen miles from *anything!* This creek is under lease to the lodge, so it gets very little pressure.

Located in a poor man's Grand Canyon, it is a mixture of deep bends, quick riffles, and flat glides that will reduce you to tears with the technical difficulty of catching a trout from its mysterious depths. We had a good day, in perfect weather, and agreed the drive was worth it. I spent a worthwhile hour at a pool that Pete later told me is called Train Wreck Bend by the locals, for the very good reason that a grain train jumped the tracks there in the mid-1980s, killing several people, and causing some consternation among the ranchers, as the deer and bear became increasingly intoxicated on the fermented grain strewn in the wreck's path.

This is only half a mile from a tall sandstone ledge above the creek known as Buffalo Jump. It seems that the Sioux would chase a herd of buffalo off the cliff, and then harvest the remains. Crude, but effective. This is high mountain, semiarid country, and nothing comes easy.

I had a conference call scheduled for the evening, so we got back to the lodge by seven p.m. Jim Wolf left me like a bad habit, as there was a caddis hatch of some intensity starting, and cutthroat trout were rising along the bank. Can't say I blame him.

FRIDAY, JULY 4, 2003

Friday, the Fourth of July, was a picture perfect high mountain morning, crisp, clear, and invigorating. We were too agitated to enjoy breakfast, and departed early to stake our claim to a prime section of Armstrong's Creek, a mere eight miles from the lodge. Pete, our guide, is a tall, lanky, fishing fool. He has the westerner's laconic habits, but what he says is worth listening to…for example, we pulled into the parking area, put on our waders, assembled our plunder, grabbed our rods, and headed for the stream. As he opened the gate to the stream, he turned back to us with glint in his eye and said, "Welcome to Disneyland." And so it was.

We fished the same section, with a short break for lunch, for 11 hours. Jim's normal demeanor is that of a squirrel on tequila, but he brings an intimidating intensity to his fishing. He took at least 5 fish without moving his feet. I was equally fixated. During the day both Jim and I probably netted 25 fish each, between 15 and 20 inches. Mostly rainbows, but some browns, and the occasional cutbow hybrid. When you get tennis elbow from catching trout, you are having fun.

Armstrong's showed Pete to his best advantage. When we first waded out, we could see rising fish surrounding us, but no takers. "Try this," Pete murmured. Nope. "Wonder if they are taking this," he said. Nope. "OK, I see what they are taking," he said.

Then we caught fish pretty steadily all day long. Now, this is a good trick. You might not think there is much difference between a Pale-Morning Dun, and a Pale-Evening Dun, but a trout does. A creature with a brain the size of half a dried pea is smarter than you are when it comes to matters such as this. They can tell the difference between a two-tailed, greenish—yellow bug and a three tailed yellowish-green bug, when experts have to get out the magnifying glass. And if your tippet (basically a cob-web that ties your fly to your line) shows...forget it!

Trout have a built-in calendar, and they know what time it is, all the time. You may catch fish in April, throwing a fly that doesn't hatch 'til late June, but not many. John Gierach calls them "fish that just want to get caught." Too bad there are not more of them around. A trout is not very smart, but he's smarter than you are.

Speaking of smart, I skipped the mumbled invitation to accompany Jim and Pete to the Fourth of July rodeo celebration in Livingston that evening. One of the few nice things about get-ting older is that you develop a nose for trouble, and if ever I smelled trouble, this was it. The boys managed to conceal their glee that they would not have to babysit the old guy, and beat a hasty retreat for the festivities.

For my own part, I was happy to have dinner with Steven Ambrose's book about George Armstrong Custer, and Crazy Horse. "Not a bad night," I thought to myself, as the wind died down on the patio overlooking the river, the medium-rare sirloin arrived, the final scotch in my glass attained breathability, the sun touched the peaks of the Absarokas on the other side of the val-ley, and the Buena Vista Social Club played in the background. I had reached the part in the book where Custer was stationed at Fort Riley, Kansas.

Now ordinarily this would bring a sense of kinship with the subject, as I was raised on the back side of the military reservation there, and know those short grass prairies well. I remember the house on Officer's Row that Custer lived in while stationed there. Eisenhower's Kansas experiences make me feel closer to him as a person, as they parallel my own experience, but not so with Custer. I mean, the man was an idiot. Bill Steinkraus talks about Second Lieutenants on the .45 pistol range at Ft. Riley in 1942, shooting their own horses while at the gallop. But hell, they were Second Lieutenants, and I never thought there was anything dumber, until I read this part of the book. Here we have a Major General who leaves his command in hostile country to go hunting, gets lost, decides it doesn't matter anyway, goes galloping across the plains after a buffalo, and nails his own horse right between the ears with a .44 slug. Idiot.

Saturday, July 5, 2003

Speaking of idiots, did I mention that Jim and Pete went to the rodeo last night? When I woke up on Saturday morning, I knew I was going to hear some lies today. "How could you tell?" you well might ask, "Was it the accumulation of years of experience in a variety of cultures?" "No," I would reply, "it was the fact that Jim's bed was empty." That was my first clue that they had had so much to drink that they had laid down where Jesus flung 'em. They surfaced shortly thereafter, looking decidedly shopworn. I have seen better looking road kill. I knew it was bad when Jim did not even want any coffee, on the grounds that the smell made him nauseous.

The boys were wounded but game, so we headed for the Yellowstone River, known to the local trout bums as "the stone." The sun came up, the fresh air started to work its magic (that happens, when you are under 40), and the truth started to gradually emerge, like odor off a dead groundhog. It appears that the boys started out at the rodeo. You have to buy a ticket for the rodeo. With me so far? Jim surfaced from the line a few dollars poorer and a blue ink admission stamp on his hand. Oooops, I thought you were going to get your own stamp, Pete. No problem, I will just lick the back of my hand, roll it off on your hand, and away we go. First, it does not speak well of Jim, to stoop to such skullduggery (the last time I heard of that trick was just before they switched to ultraviolet ink at the Tulagi, Boulder, Colorado, 1963.) Next, it greatly lessens one's chances of a short-term interpersonal relationship. I mean, it takes all the buzz out of it when a good looking girl bursts out "Eeeeewh, dude, you gotta blue tongue!"

One of the last collective memories I elicited from Frick and Frack is of watching the Fourth of July fire works in Livingston from the roof of Dan Bailey's Fly Shop...kinda like Christmas with the Pope on the porch.

"I never shoulda had those last three tequila shooters," Jim finally admitted. In vino veritas.

I think I am starting to have too much fun out here...I'd better get back to work, or the next thing you know, I'll be tying my own flies. Hope you had as much fun reading this as I did living through it. See you soon.

LIKE CHOCOLATE FOR TROUT

I am suspended in yet another aluminum tube at 37,000 feet, but this time it is for pleasure, not work, as I am on my way home from a fishing trip to the Green River in Dutch John, Utah. (That's some map book you have, if you can find it!) Dutch John is in the Three Corners area, where the borders of Colorado, Wyoming, and Utah join.

I went with Paul and Todd Seymour, which was tremendous fun. Paul has caught fish in two hemispheres and on three continents, and Todd has been a professional guide and can catch big fish in wet grass, when every one else is getting skunked. To say that I was sharpening my hooks and cleaning my line does not begin to describe it. This was some serious fishing company. Add to that the fact that we are family, and you can imagine the chatter was pretty spicy!

This is the time of year on the Green River when the cicada hatch happens, and trout aficionados come to take advantage of the trout's taking leave of their senses. The cicada locusts come in two varieties—the seven- and the seventeen-year version. I can tell the difference, but only just. Basically, one has some orange on it, and one doesn't. As near as I can make out, their sole purpose in life is to lie in the earth at the base of a tree, hatch in their seventh, or seventeenth year, depending, emerge from their pupa, roost in the trees for a week or so, mate, deposit their larvae in the bark of the same or similar tree, then fly onto the surface of the river to commit suicide in the jaws of a trout. Mother Nature is a tricky old lady, isn't she?

These bugs hatch from late May to mid-June every year. They are about the size of your thumb, and have vaguely the same effect that chocolate is reputed to have on those who partake. Trout of enormous size and venerable condition are seen to abandon all caution under these circumstances, much to the gratification of a serious amateur trout bum such as myself. When a 24-inch, 4-pound brown trout takes your fly and leaves the water the length of his body to do so, it makes your heart stop. The next trout that I lift my rod tip on too high and too soon won't be the first. These creatures make you jumpy!

The Green is a tail-water fishery, so the conditions are nearly perfect for trout...cold, clean water, lots of bugs on a regular schedule, and fresh water shrimp, called "scuds" as a steady diet. The first section of the river, just below the Flaming Gorge Dam, has a reputed 15,000 trout per mile, dropping to "only" 5,000 in the lower section. That works out to about one trout for every one and one half feet of river bottom! There are a lot of fish in this river. Fortunately, a lot of them are also very dumb at this time of year. We landed between fifteen and twenty trout every day we were out.

It does not hurt that all this takes place in the Rockies, with all the scenery and weather that implies. We were lucky, as we had low seventies every day, mostly sunshine; and the daily violent, towering thunderstorms slid around us the whole time we were there. There is a lot of history around here, as Americans measure such things. My first day on the river, we put our boat in at the Jarvis ranch, where Butch Cassidy and the Sundance Kid used to hide out between their raids. Whatever they were making robbing banks wasn't enough, as far as I can see, as the social life in Dutch John leaves quite a lot to the imagination, even today. One hundred and ten years ago, there would have been only so many times one could read the Montgomery Ward catalogue...besides; it was probably being put to other use in the outhouse. The original owner made his living running a ferry service across the Green, which was a considerable body of water, before being somewhat domesticated by the dam up river.

In between the Jarvis ranch and Dutch John are the log cabin remains of a Pony Express way station. "Young, tough, hardy young men wanted," says the Pony Express poster offering employment as riders, "orphans preferred." There is something to be said for truth in advertising, after all. If you want to see the future of snail mail now that the Internet is here, take a look at Clay Flats, Utah.

Fishing aside, which was only fabulous, the main impression I took away from my travels is of the immense distances involved in the American West. It took tough people, the Jim Bridgers Jeremiah Johnsons, and Kit Carsons of the world to ride some square withered cow pony with short, straight pasterns through that expanse. I have read a lot about that era, and the romance of it comes through all right, but most writers miss the back-breaking, grinding labor it took to ensure daily existence. The smell of mesquite wood smoke and the sight of purple hills of sage brush in the Rocky Mountain twilight are all very well, but it would have been tough to appreciate it when you were riding 20 miles a day on dried pinto beans and rancid bacon. Tough people. I think I would rather look down on it from here than live it.

Hope you are all well, and I will talk to you soon...when I feel my lies have progressed sufficiently to be told in polite company.

NO GREENHORNS ON THE GREEN

July 19, 2004

Enter stage left, laughing. I had just arrived in Salt Lake City after teaching a riding clinic in Northern California on my way to the Green River. Passing by Gate B-2, I had a sudden flashback to meeting my nephew, John Seymour, at that gate, several years ago. We were meeting up for a family trip to the Smith River, and I had arrived at the gate in good time and was reading a book.

Something caught my eye, and when I looked up, I saw the most hungover human being I have ever seen, outside of a mirror. John Seymour had been up to something, and it had caught up with him. Being the master of understatement that I am, I thought to myself, "John doesn't look too good." On a scale of 1 to 10, this one was about an 89. He flopped down into the seat next to me and said, "Oh, Favorite Uncle, I think I broke my propeller."

"Uh-huh," I said, "what's her name?" (He was single at the time.)

"I don't want to talk about it," he said.

This was the same trip that Tim Dudley got off one of his classic lines about me. The float down the Smith coincided with Gail and my thirtieth wedding anniversary, and that night, surrounded by friends and family, and looking at the million-dollar sky over our heads, I raised my glass of all purpose brown to the heavens, and said, "Just think, boys, 30 years ago tonight we were married, and she loves me so much, she let me go on the trip of a lifetime over our anniversary."

Dudley's dry retort was, "Hell, she thought that was your present to her!"

Anyway, that was then and this is now. Still, there is no use having memories if you don't drag them out again every once in a while, and amuse yourself all over again. I laughed all the way out of the airport, turned left towards the Rockies, and headed for Dutch John, Utah.

Coming out of the Echo River valley, you climb up on the plateau above Wahstach. There is a moment across the top when you have a 360-degree view. That's a hell of a view, I thought to myself. Too bad there's nothing to see. This part of Utah and Wyoming is pretty barren. If you look north, there is nothing between you and the Arctic Circle but one strand of barbed wire that some white supremacy wing nuts have strung up above Coeur d'Alene. You have to wonder what brought Jim Bridger and the other mountain men out this way. Just thinking about riding over this vast expanse of nothing makes your piles hurt. And they didn't have two-ply Charmin, either.

It is a strange sensation, looking ahead and saying, "It's going to rain in about an hour."

You can do that because you can see the weather for hours ahead. It is going to change if you wait a little while, but the scenery won't. We are talking barren here.

Of course, mankind has screwed it up a fair bit too. Any time you see signs about Westvaco, or Sechrist Chemical, you might as well put some EPA tape around it. Every half an hour or so, you will drive past some lunar 'scape, with a plume of smoke and noxious fumes streaming down wind. Signs of progress.

A lot of the land out here is what is called "open range." This means that agribusiness is allowed to overgraze public land. The rancher's rule of thumb is 25 acres of land per cow, but all I can say is that there are some scraggledy-ass longhorns hereabouts. It is hard to raise stock when there is nothing around but sage brush, and tumble weed.

By this time, I still had over 200 miles to go, so I handled all this the only way you can...I knocked the top off a 20-ounce Diet Coke, ripped open the Cheetos, plugged in a live Little Feat CD, and took a buggy whip to my jelly bean shaped rent-a-wreck. It's the only solution.

After two hours east on I-80, or two lifetimes, whichever comes first, you turn south on 191 at Rock Springs, Wyoming. I love the place names out here. Westerners don't BS you about life in the northern plains...when you hear about places like Bitter Creek, Salt Creek Road, or the Fire Hole, you don't have much doubt what things are like.

I also like Westerner's laconic, understated sense of humor. Just after you turn south at Rock Springs, you pass a big yellow highway sign that says, "Drifting Snow Possible." Just behind the sign is a 20-foot high snow drift barrier made out of steel highway guard rails. Portions of this steel drift fence are crumpled and broken, due to the weight of last years' snow drifts. That is some serious wind and snow. Of course if you wait six months, it will be 110 degrees in the shade. By then the only shade for miles around will be under the steel drift fence, but you gotta go with what you've got.

A little closer to the Flaming Gorge, things start to green up a little, and you can see deer and the occasional elk grazing along the foothills. It was only about 150 years ago that over 60 million buffalo covered most of these plains, but the cowboys and buffalo hunters took care of that problem. Too bad we can't get some of these western good ol' boys to play "Cowboys and Islamofascists."

If they could do half the job that they did on the buffalo, we wouldn't need the French after all.

I pulled into the parking lot of the Flaming Gorge Lodge about 4:30 p.m., checked in, and lugged my considerable fishing plunder inside. You gotta love it when a plan comes together. The phone rang, and it was Peter Howell, five minutes away, and looking for a fishing report.

"What in the world were you doing, hanging around with miscreants like Peter Howell and Todd Seymour?" you might ask. You met Pete in an earlier chapter, and Todd is one of my nephews, and a serious fisherman.

Well, on the one hand, you are known by the company you keep. But on the other hand, you have to understand that it is hard for me to find a group of guys that can make me look good. Where else could a fella come in first *and* third in the 2004 Patagonia Wader-Odor Contest, and have someone around that he could brag about it to? I mean, I need these guys.

Pete had mentioned that he was bringing a friend, and I had said yeah, OK, and thought no more about it. So, I was startled when I looked into Pete's truck, and got my face licked by Brutus, a Welsh Springer spaniel. Brute is a cute guy, and all about fishing. My calls to Todd Seymour had gone unanswered, so I told Pete, "He's floating the 'A section,' and won't be back until dark. We gotta go and catch some fish."

We drove to the Little Hole parking lot and walked upriver, where we proceeded to get the skunk off. Leaving at dark, we met Todd for a little all purpose brown, followed by a quick steak dinner, and an eight-hour nap.

There is no hustle and bustle like that of a bunch of grown men, preparing to act like children for the day. There is an air of feverish expectation, and furious activity, mixed with profanity and testosterone in equal proportions. Bags are rummaged through, rods are inspected, waders are packed, and various essential and nonessential items are forgotten and remembered. Eventually it all works itself out, and the boys can head for the river.

The A section of the Green is as full of fish as ever, and today we all caught our share. Todd shared his secrets about catching fish here. Basically you float down river to a likely looking bank, park your boat, and head back upstream. You creep along, searching quite close to the banks for signs of a trout. Watching Todd, I had the image of a blue heron stalking fish. He fishes with a short line and infinite patience, and that patience is usually rewarded. Before you know it, he had all of us stalking, and catching, fish.

"I'm going to call this the Green River Crane step," I thought. It looks funny, but it sure works. Fishing will humble you. I was watching Toddy, doing the Green River Crane step, when he hooked into a big fish. Now picture this: I was looking back up the magnificent Flaming Gorge. Sunlight sparkling on the river, bright blue skies, the whole picture. "I need a photo of this," I thought, and grabbed for my camera. In the meantime, I let my rod, and fly, dangle behind me, while I grappled with the Nikon.

"What's that funny tug?" You guessed it...a 24-inch brown trout had snuck up on my fly while it dangled behind, and ambushed it. Pete heard the commotion, and came running with his net, and helped me land it. When I described the sequence of events he just smiled. I could hear him thinking "luck beats skill every time."

After the usual alarums and excursions at the takeout point, we headed home, so as to rest up and prepare for another day of fishing. Todd is great company for me. His politics make me look like a liberal (he thinks Ann Coulter is a little bit of a softie), and he is the most independent cuss you could ever hope to meet. Over a glass of brown, Pete and I made noises about floating a different part of the river on the following morning. I had already gathered that Todd was going back to the A section again, but I amused myself by gently trying to get him to change his mind and float with us. Not gonna happen. Once Todd makes up his mind, he's got a street named after him, and it's called "One Way." But you have to hand it to him; he was always polite, while he was telling me to take a hike. My kind of guy.

So on Wednesday, Pete and I decided to float the B section, based on the excellent logic that neither one of us had ever seen it before. Todd, of course, smiled and said he would stick with what he knew. We caught some fish, but the experience was not the same as the day before. Pete did catch one cutthroat that had the most extraordinary colors, like an illustration by James Prosek on acid.

At the end of the day, after about two seconds discussion, we both agreed that we would not pester the fish on this section again. To top off the day, Pete had to row the last mile and a half, which made me feel badly for him. Not bad enough to take a turn on that infernal contraption, but I did at least feel his pain, you gotta give me that.

We split up, and Pete headed for points north, while I headed back to Salt Lake City for an early flight to Gunnison, Colorado. There I met Gail, and we drove to Valley View Ranch, in Lake City, CO. I was out of sorts, as United had once again lost my luggage, but the thought of spending a few days with Gail in the Rockies was enough to repair my ill-humor and surly attitude.

Kathie and Ed Cox come up from Texas to their ranch near Lake City, Colorado, for the summer to escape the heat, and basically preside over a Disneyland for grown-ups. Hiking, fishing, riding, historical tours, it's all here. Add to that wonderful cabins, five-star cuisine, and an incredible array and variety of guests, and it all makes for quite an experience.

The fishing is the big plus for me, as the Cox's stretch of the Gunnison is by far the best river I have ever experienced. I typically go into a fishing frenzy when I get here, which lasts for the duration of our stay. Ed and Kathie know this about me, as they have caught my act before. After a lunch by the river, everyone was choosing their afternoon activities. When Kathie got to me, she just stopped and made a shooing motion with her hand. I was off like a rocket, and spent an afternoon up to my waist in the Gunnison River.

It's funny now, but that night, as we were getting ready for dinner, it was no joke. I heard Gail calling me. You know how you can tell when some one is not kidding? Like that. I turned the corner on a 45-degree tilt at a high rate of speed, to find that her hair dryer had slipped out of her hand, and was busily churning the water to froth in the toilet.

"So," I thought, "it's like a toilet Jacuzzi. I guess if you are having problems with whatever, you could just...OK, OK, no time for potty humor right now."

"Don't just stand there," said Gail, "do something."

I made a quick tour around the cabin, but to no avail. "You can never find a circuit breaker when you need one," I muttered. No sparks were coming out of the toilet yet, but I figured it was only a matter of time.

The dryer had not submerged the motor part, but was busily whipping the surface of the water in the bowel into a toilet-smoothie. There was an ominous burning smell, and I was a little leery of grabbing hold of an instrument that could conceivably short circuit my pacemaker.

After a couple of false starts, I finally pulled the hair dryer out by reaching in with a kitchen chair, much like a lion tamer, and flipping it out onto the bathroom floor. No harm done, once our pulses subsided. I wiped it dry, and handed it back to her.

"What do you think?" Gail asked.

"Go ahead and use it," I said. "Just try not to think about where it's been."

Fortunately, the hair dryer escapade did not affect my fishing-jones, and the next morning saw me ready to go again. Ed has placed structures in the river every 50 yards or so, to provide cover for the fish. The fish have repaid him by thriving and propagating. I have never seen so many big fish in such good condition. And aggressive, too. Put your fly in the water, and a duck on a June bug has nothing on these fish.

When I fish, I don't keep track of exactly how many I catch. It seems like a waste of time, since I'm going to put them back anyway. John Gierach says there are only three possible outcomes when you fish...you either catch none, a few, or a bunch. I caught a bunch, including one Snake River cutthroat that had to be 26-inches long, the biggest cutthroat I have ever caught.

The afternoon of our last day there, Ed took me almost to the top of Silver Mountain above Trophy Lake. Pointing into the canyon, which has a long, steep, circuitous trail down to Ghost Town, he said, "No one has been on Larson's Creek in two years due to the weather up here. Basically you hike down there, and follow the new trail back up to the road crossing, fishing for Snake River cutthroats all the way back up. It's only about a mile, straight up hill. Tell me what the new trail is like, and give me a report on how my fish are doing. You got it?"

"Sure," I said, thinking that I was not going to have to get on the treadmill that afternoon. It was in the cards that this mountain was going to put a whipping on me. As Ed pulled away, he had a small smile on his face, like he was thinking, "OK, that'll fix Isaac Walton for quite a while, now let's go see what my other dudes are up to."

The background to this little jaunt is that every time I come out to Valley View Ranch, Ed and I hike up Larson's Creek, and do an informal fish survey. The first time we did this, almost 10 years ago, the fish population was about two-thirds Snake River cutthroats, and one-third brook trout. This was not good news from Ed's point of view. We took out all the brookies as we caught them, in an attempt to gentrify the neighborhood.

The cutthroats are the original inhabitants of this watershed, having moved in right after the Pleistocene Era, discovered that they were in the fish version of Fat City, and had been there ever since. Sometime in the late 1800s the local gold miners around what is now known as Ghost Town had decided to "improve" Larson's Creek, and they released the brookies into the creek, where the two species had maintained an uneasy coexistence ever since.

Of course, the miners never stopped to think that the raw sewage that they were adding to the sluice water coming out of their silver mine might have something to do with the decline in the water quality.

"How did they know silver was there?" you might ask. Simple. They would just dynamite entire mountain faces, and poke through the rubble like grave robbers, picking over the bones of a better time. Dynamite. Entire mountain faces. All over the Rockies. Progress.

Anyway, I was bound and determined to see how the trout were doing in the creek, since I felt a vaguely proprietary concern for them. Trout are the coal mine canary of watersheds, and I thought I might see for myself how our planet is doing in this little corner of the cosmos. As usual, the answer is both good news and bad news. The good news is that the brookies are gone. The bad news is that the recent drought has affected the population of cutthroats, and they are scarce right now. But there is a range in the size of the fish, and the ones that I caught are feisty and healthy. If we don't flush any more raw sewage down the creek for a while, they are going to be OK.

By the end of the afternoon, I had stopped fishing, and contented myself with watching each likely pool for signs of movement. I had been able to return all the fish I had caught safely to the creek, but I was worried I might mishandle one. They are too pretty, and too scarce, to take a chance. Cutthroats have to be opportunistic, so if you wait for a few minutes, and they are there, you'll see them. Not every likely pool held a fish, but enough to reassure me that they are still around after all those years.

I was intent enough that I was surprised when I looked up, and saw the road up ahead of me. Turning towards home, I stopped to catch my breath at the top of a curve. I knew I was going to have to do that several times on the climb out of the canyon, and thought I might as well get in the habit. I felt a vague sense of regret as I took my last look back down into the canyon. I had been happy down there, and I was returning to a more complicated world. But it was time to go, so I turned uphill and kept walking towards my waiting car.

Curiosity is a powerful urge with me. I have to admit that one thing that led me back to the ranch was a recollection that at lunch there had been rumors of a volleyball game, and hints of margaritas in the air.

"Margaritas would be like coals to Newcastle with this bunch," I thought. "I wonder how they are doing?"

As soon as I stepped out of the car, I knew how they were doing....well. Very well indeed. Every few minutes a roar would drift up from the volleyball court.

"I wonder if that is what the Coliseum sounded like in ancient Rome?"

At any rate, everybody was having a good time by this time. The mood carried on into dinner, where we had a raucous send-off party. The proceedings were enlightened by one young lady's recounting of her and her husband's first Valentine's Day together. She had decided to give her new husband a Valentine's Day present he would not soon forget, and had been to Victoria's Secret where she purchased a Valentine's Day, uuuhhh, costume. She hid in the closet to await his arrival. Imagine her surprise when he pulled open the door to the downstairs closet, saying, "Hi, honey, I brought my boss home for dinner."

The laughter died down eventually, but it took a while.

There were more stories in this vein, but I'm not sure I should put them down, as John Ashcroft's censors might disapprove.

Towards the end of the evening, I wandered outside for a breath of fresh air, and looked up into a million dollar Colorado nighttime sky. Stars everywhere, and not a cloud in the sky. Earlier today Steven Hawking had announced a change in his famous black hole theory.

"I hope I'm around when they finally figure it out," I thought. "I am kind of curious about how all this got started, and where it will wind up."

Which brings me back to why Jim Bridger came out into this part of the world in the first place? I guess he came out for the same reason I hiked down into Lawson's Creek. He was curious. My curiosity keeps me on the road a great deal and that gets a bit wearisome, so I'm going back to Fox Covert now. I think I have three grandsons these days, but I can't make them hold still long enough to count. I'll just count the legs as they go by and divide by two. If it comes out even, that means I was close enough. Anyway, it does me good to have them around.

What part will I remember the best? I dunno, that story at dinner will be hard to beat. But then there is that big fish I caught by holding my rod backwards, while I was trying to take a picture of Todd. And don't forget the toilet Jacuzzi. And...what was that? Did you hear that? Did you see that? I wonder what that was. I gotta go now. Exit stage right, laughing.

THE MUD
MARCH

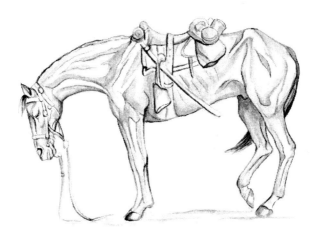

I have always loved history. I think part of it is the interesting people that you learn about, and another part of it is that I live in an area that is replete with historical significance. The farm that we have lived on for 35 years is the part of the site of the Battle of Upperville, which took place June 18, 1863. If you look along the old stone walls, you can still find bits of metal, buttons, bullets, and other fragments of the fight, and when I first moved here, old-timers showed me the mound next door, on Ayreshire Farm, where the dead horses and mules from that battle were buried. I can see that mound from my window, and I can see the road that a very young George Washington used to take, as he set out to survey the Western Territories for Lord Fairfax. On the one hand, these things happened a long time ago. On the other hand, they are still all around us; we just have to look for them.

When I drive south along the Piedmont to go duck hunting on the Rappahannock River, I parallel the routes that the Union and Confederate forces used in their marches during the Civil War. One of those marches went down in history as the Mud March. I was thinking about that march as I drove down that way recently, and the following chapter is the result of that journey

This Friday, January 20, I will be sitting on the bank of the Rappahannock River with my Labrador, Nacho. The duck hunting is not very good any more, so I will have plenty of time to sit in the mud, and think. The forecast is for rain, and this is as it should be. One thing I will be thinking is that this is the 143rd anniversary of the infamous Mud March, which the Army of the Potomac made, beginning early in the morning, January 20, 1863. I consider those days a bit, and try to see the lessons that are shrouded in so much time now, and so many words, and not enough thought. The Army of the Potomac was the unluckiest of all armies. All armies are by definition unlucky, as their existence speaks of the failure of men who should be smarter, and wiser, than to plunge their young men into war. But of all those unlucky armies, the Army of the Potomac was the unluckiest: unlucky in its organization and location, unlucky in having to fight a war between brothers, and most of all, unlucky in its Generals. At that time Ambrose Burnside was the Commanding General, Burnside of the pleasant demeanor, and the flamboyant side whiskers, and the all too human failures, and of a surprising organizational skill, and of the tragic inability to believe in his men, and himself. He was wrong about many things, but he was prescient in one thing. When he accepted the command of the Army, he told Lincoln that he feared he would not be up to it. He was right in that, and his boys would pay the price, again and again. Weeden later remarked that the Army was cursed "by a line of brave and patriotic officers whom some good fairy should have knocked on the head." But good fairies were in short supply just then, and Lee would do all the hard knocking any man could stand.

Early that morning the Army bestirred itself. Its camps stretched from below Ferry Farm, George Washington's farm on the east bank of the Rappahannock, several miles north to US Ford, and Ealy's Ford, all the way to Germana Ford. The rear area and supply lines of the Army went back to the Potomac River, to Aquia Landing and Belle Plain. By now all the terrain in those parts was denuded of trees, as the men had cut all the trees for firewood and timber. Soldiers and officers alike, they burned everything they could get their hands on. Mary Parke Custis Lee, the grand daughter of George Washington and the wife of Robert E. Lee, had left her ancestral home at Arlington. The Union troops stationed there gleefully burned the fence rails, the furniture, and even the moldings and window frames. Soon enough, her garden east of the mansion down to the Potomac would become the site for a very different sort of digging and planting.

When you drive through Loudoun and Fauquier Counties these days and notice cedar trees, you can be sure that the scene was populated by Civil War troops, for cedar loves fallow ground, and the Army's insatiable need for wood had left nothing in its wake but fallow ground. Study an old photo sometime, taken from the hill in Warrenton just North of Moseby's house and looking northwest towards Bear Wallow Road and the old Gold Cup course. As far as you can see in that photo, the woods are gone, and the fields are bare of fencing, and the wastage of war is manifest. But cedar, the weed of war, found a home.

Burnside's plan was a good one. March north along the river, cross quickly, get around Lee's left flank, take Richmond, and the war would be over. But it was going to be hard to march in the mud, and impossible to do anything quickly, so the plan was not going to work. At this time the Army numbered over 130,000 men, for the terrible losses of December's Battle of Fredericksburg had been made good, if the senseless slaughter of many thousands of boys can be made good. It was bitter cold, and had been raining for days, and nothing was easy. The soil along the river in those parts is a mixture of clay and sand, and either one becomes impassable under heavy rain: when combined they produce a viscous, miserable, slimy mixture that defies passage. Yet orders are orders, and the soldiers (boys, really—their manhood waited for them down the road) moved off in the dark. But the rain came harder, and the bottom dropped out of the roads, and the cannon sank to their hubs and horses and mules died in their traces, and were cut from their harness where they fell, and were trampled into the mud and disappeared, merely some of the two and a half million horses and mules that died during the war.

Men came in with ropes to do the work of the fallen animals, sometimes hundreds of men to a cannon, but it was all to no avail. An army is a hard thing to move, and once it is on the move it takes a great deal to make it stall, but now it stalled. The rain came even harder, and thousands of boots churned impassible mud to impossible depths, and Generals fumed, and Colonels shouted, and Sergeants swore, and the Fords flooded. The Army would flounder for another day and a night, but it was all no good.

Fatigue came on, and disappointment, and, naturally, rage. In that Army, the soldiers were served a whiskey ration, and the wagons containing this precious cargo were on the march along with the soldiers, and boys will be boys. Cheap commissary whiskey hit empty stomachs, and one thing led to another, and soldiers who had been nerved to a life or death struggle with Lee's men across the river now avenged real or imagined slights with neighboring regiments. So the 118th Pennsylvania and the 22nd Massachusetts tangled, and arbitrated their differences with fists and kicks, and the 2nd Maine came in to play the peace-maker. No good deed goes unpunished, and the Mainers were soon giving as good as they got. Peace and military order were reestablished, but only by the hardest, and the regiments were no use to themselves or anybody else, and finally the orders to return to camp sifted down through the ranks.

It was not easy to see anything good in all this, and the Army generally agreed that it had been a monumental failure, but the thing to notice is that those boys made the final determination, for they stayed in the ranks, and they complained, and tormented their neighbors in the next tent with pranks, and tried to stay warm and dry. Their mud march was over, but they stayed. At this distance it is impossible to know what kept them. The metaphor could not have been plainer, of an Army, and a policy of war, and a government, and a nation, mired in the mud. Yet they stayed, and endured, and finally, hundreds of days and thousands of dead boys later, they stood in long ranks, and watched Bobby Lee ride away from Appomattox.

Burnside would be supplanted by then, and Meade, until Lincoln found a man in U. S. Grant, who, in his chilling phrase, "understands the arithmetic." And a war that had been started for one reason was won for another, and it may be that the privates understood this better than their officers, that the limited, gallant, chivalrous war as it began could not be maintained, for the Emancipation Proclamation had been promulgated, and now it was not a war of restoration, but a war of good against evil. Not all had thought it so, and not all the soldiers agreed, and not all the politicians, but it had become a hard war, and the boys of the Army of the Potomac had become hard men, and it may be they saw it clear. There would be no compromise with those who would hold another man in servitude. There would be hard fighting, and battle scenes beyond belief or description, but there could be only one answer, and that answer was freedom.

It comes to me, sitting on the bank of the Rappahannock in the mud that the times now are much as they were. A nation at war, begun for one reason, now changing and expanding. A divided nation, with all the crosscurrents and subplots that human nature can ever produce. But both wars became a war between good and evil, and not all agreed then or now that the war was right, or good, or even necessary. Democracies are slow to hate, but they learn, and they become adept at it, and willing to lay waste to all before them, in order to destroy the evil which hates the good.

And Lincoln and Bush each steered their course, while men from both parties, of good and high minds or corrupt and venal nature, quarreled and schemed all around them. Now again the very existence of evil is debated and denied and accepted, and men of good character take an opposing stance, and men of low character take advantage, and we have seen all of this before. One can find similarities between Clement Vanlandingham and Howard Dean, men who do not see the chasm of treason at their feet while they look to their stars. In the meantime, hard war men rise to their stations, and Edwin Stanton and Dick Cheney would have much in common, and much to agree on. And the only things we can be sure of are that we are at war, and we are unsure of the outcome. Yet it is a wonderful thing to be free, and we must do what we can.

From where Nacho and I sit, the early morning fog on the river looks like wood smoke from the campfires of the Army of the Potomac, and gun smoke from the battles that decided things, and the Rappahannock rolls by, inexorable as freedom.

PART II

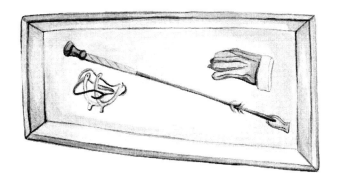

MOSTLY HORSES

COWBOY MARDI GRAS

THURSDAY, MAY 19, 2005

You can't believe everything you read in the paper. On the other hand, the minute I read that newspaper article about the Miles City Bucking Horse Sale, I knew I had to go. I mean, anything that bills itself as "The Cowboy Mardi Gras" needs investigation. Bucking horses, cowboys, loud music, Miles City has it all. Needless to say, Gail was under-whelmed when I mentioned the prospect, and it was only the intervention of our friends, Nina and Ned Bonnie, that saved me. How bad could it be, if they were going to come along?

"I guess I had better wait to break the news about the four of us staying in a 29-foot RV," I thought to myself. "She's a pioneer woman, she can handle it "

The best way to get there is to fly in to Billings, pick up your home-on-wheels for the week and hit the interstate. Flying these days is not so bad except for the security. All those TSA (Thousands Standing Around) security types make me nervous. Gail doesn't do dirt, so I amused myself watching her, trading her shoes for flip-flops. Miss Tidy-Paws is *not* going to walk barefoot through the detector. Not gonna happen. Of course it could be worse. Just think where we would be if Richard Reid had hidden that bomb in a suppository. "You want me to *what?*"

Anyway, it is about three hours to Miles City, and it is an interesting drive. You pass by Indian sites and battle monuments, and as soon as you get past the Billings city limits, the land is covered with winter wheat, horses, and cattle.

Driving east over the Rosebud River brought that jackass George Armstrong Custer to my mind. The Battle of the Little Big Horn was fought near here, and the countryside still looks pretty much the same. You half expect to see the U. S. Seventh Cavalry come trotting around the next hill. Of course they would not have been up to full strength. At that time Custer's unit had the highest desertion rate of any mounted unit in the United States. The seventh troopers were not very smart (most of them did not have an eighth grade education) but they were smart enough to figure out that while they might get whipped or shot for desertion, that damn fool Custer was going to get them killed for certain. As it turns out, he did a good job of it. Custer was a glory-hunting egomaniac, and profligate with the lives of his men, so naturally those ninnies in Congress built a memorial in his honor. I'd better change the subject; I can feel a fit coming on.

The scenery changes during the drive. It starts out as classic Rocky Mountain and winds up as springtime-green high altitude prairie. Miles City isn't the Bad Lands, but you can see them from here, and you sense the potential for extreme weather...110 in the summer, with the countryside sere, cracked, and parched;

50 below in the winter, wind, mud, ice, dangerous roads, or as on this week end, glorious spring sunshine and cobalt skies.

By this time we pulled into the KOA campgrounds ("Why, yes, Dear, we are staying here. Oh, but I thought I had told you.") Anyway, no scar, no story. The Bonnies arrived safely, but an early night seemed like a good idea, so pizza and bed.

FRIDAY, MAY 20, 2005

The festivities did not officially start until 12:30. This gave us time to wander around the Range Riders Museum for a couple of hours and soak up the history and culture of the area. The museum is a cornucopia of history. It has displays of the various tools that the settlers used on a daily basis, ranging from nineteenth century farrier's tools (which are remarkably similar to present-day tools) to an entire wing dedicated to buckboards, chuck wagons, and military vehicles of various descriptions.

I got my first hint that this trip would not be all fun and games when I went into the gun room. Guns are mostly a guy thing, except for Ann Coulter, who says, "A Glock is a girl's best friend." The museum has hundreds of handguns and rifles on display, so naturally I was stuck there for a while. What especially drew my attention was a badly rusted handgun that had been found on the site of the Battle of the Little Big Horn. I wondered which one of the poor unfortunates who followed that idiot Custer carried this pistol, and what he was thinking when he used it for the last time. The veteran's advice to the rookie troopers was, "Save the last one for yourself." The point being, it was better to go quickly, rather than staked out over an ant hill. The vibes off that old rusted pistol were pretty strong, so you can understand why I was a bit spooked by the time I left the gun room.

The museum has a marvelous collection of photographs of both settlers and natives. Some of the photos of the natives are amazingly evocative. While it is true that a picture is worth a thousand words, all thousand of them can be lies. At the same time, these photos capture the essence of many of the subjects. Red Cloud could be dressed up in a Brooks Brothers suit, and pass for a CEO. Chief Joseph, who led the long march of the Nez Perce towards Canada, showed wisdom, judgment, and enormous dignity. And Medicine Crow, the Absaroka war chief, was stone crazy, and to be avoided at all costs.

The last display I visited showed a 1929 black-and-white photo of the participants in a rodeo at the PK Ranch. In the foreground were about a hundred cowboys, all decked out in their biggest hats and best blue jeans. But in the background, parked on the hill, were literally hundreds of Ford Model Ts and As, bringing the Industrial Age to the West in a cloud of exhaust. The same sort of photo hangs on the wall of my stables. It shows the last mounted parade of the 10th U.S. Cavalry in 1939, before it was mechanized and sent off to war. There are troopers on horseback in the foreground, but trucks and tanks loom in the background, harbingers of progress. I thought to myself, "I'd better get out of here and find some of that cowboy Bacchanalian excess I was promised. I'm starting to think myself hinky."

It was getting on towards noon, and the crowd was moving towards the fairgrounds, so we drifted that way. Walking through the parking lot, I was struck by the range of pickup trucks assembled. Some were obviously working vehicles, covered with dust, dinged at every corner, and with cracked windshields. Others had been lovingly polished and prepared, and still others were jacked up on enormous tires, with mega boom box speakers sticking out the back, basically jukeboxes on wheels, blaring out Toby Keith, who was singing:

"We're all just killing time,
'til the Good Lord calls us home,
And the best that you can hope for is to die
with your boots on."

Now any time you have this many pickup trucks, you have a lot of pickup truck bumpers. This means you have a lot of bumper stickers. It seemed to me that the cowgirls had the best of the bumper sticker contest:

"You're spooking the horses, and you're scaring me."

"Rodeo naked."

"Save a horse. Ride a cowboy."

"Bad cowboy! Go to my room."

But the cowboys held their own:

"Gun control means using both hands."

"Rehab is for quitters."

"Say no to drugs. It leaves more time for drinking."

"Guns kill people like spoons make Rosie O'Donnell fat."

"Liberals—One a day, two in possession."

"There is room here for all God's creatures. Right next to the mashed potatoes."

I was still laughing to myself as we climbed into the bleachers. At 12:30 sharp the parade started, and it wasn't long before I had what I had come all this way for...brilliant sunshine, drunken cowboys, pretty girls in painted-on jeans, patriotic music, and horses everywhere, snorting and boogering at all the confusion. Within five minutes the Queen of the Rodeo had her saddle slip...she fell off backwards, and her horse bucked its way from front to back through the 30 or so other horses involved.

Needless to say, the rest of the horses did not take kindly to this sort of thing, and proceeded to play catch-up in the bucking department. Within seconds, the whole parade was throwing a bucking fit. Miss Horsemanship quickly landed in a cloud of dust next to the Queen of the Rodeo, and Miss Congeniality was over in the corner, snatching the crap out her horse to keep from joining them. Order was finally restored, the National Anthem was sung by the Mayor's 10-year-old daughter, and the 2005 Miles City Bucking Horse Sale was declared officially open. And not a moment too soon, either.

Underneath all the fun, some serious business is going on. They sell about 200 horses here, both "unbroken" and "spoiled saddle stock," although it is hard to tell them apart. How do you try out a bucking horse for sale? Well, you put a drunken local cowboy on it, open up the chute, and see what happens. Bucking horses generally sell for around $1,000, with the high price being about $2,000 As far as I can make out, broken arms add 500, and broken legs are worth an extra 750. Bloody noses, cuts, scrapes, and contusions don't seem to count, as they are considered the normal course of affairs around here.

The procedure is to herd a horse into an individual chute, put a saddle on it, drop a cowboy down onto its back, open up the gate, and "let her rip." The announcer here is a real pro, with a relaxed delivery and a resonant baritone that sounds like sagebrush and high mountain plains. He keeps things moving, calling the next horse and cowboy, whipping the crowd up as the pair comes out of the chute, and generally commenting on the action.

If the cowboy is sticking to his horse pretty well, he will call out, "Go uh-haid, Joe, *make* a bronc rider!" If the rider doesn't last long, he will comment, "Folks, give this cowboy uh hand, he come all the way from Sheridan, and all he's gunna take home iz yur thanks."

One cowboy was slow getting into the saddle, and obviously having second thoughts. The announcer commented dryly, "I wancha take yur time, Cody, but hurry up ev'ry chance ya git."

But my favorite line was delivered after a cowboy had been thrown in a spectacular fashion, even by Miles City standards: "That horse has more moves than uh chicken on Ex-Lax."

The pace of the sales is pretty quick. When those horses come out of the chute, they are operating in broadband, while most of the cowboys are thinking in dial-up. I swear one of those would-be bronc riders got thrown so high so fast he left his shadow behind. The instant a cowboy hits the ground, the auctioneer takes over, and starts his pitch: "Hey, now, whatta ya gonna give, whatta ya gonna give for 'im," and in less time than it takes to tell it, another horse is sold, the announcer takes over again, and yet another unfortunate is literally launched out of the next chute. They don't wait for much in Miles City...several times, the EMTs were bending over the last victim's body as the next horse was released, while a small crowd of railbirds casually waved their hands at the bronc, should he chance to buck too close to the scene of the previous accident.

The quality of the riding, and the bucking, varies enormously. This is not the Professional Rodeo Cowboys Association finals at Las Vegas, but more like semipro. Some of the horses come out and merely bounce around a little. They seem relieved when the eight-second buzzer goes, and one of the pick-up riders reaches over, and loosens the knot on the bucking strap. Some of the cowboys ride their bronc out in high style, while others are dislodged at the first buck, and bite the dust shortly thereafter.

Still, the cowboys try their best, and the horses break out of the chute like they mean business. I had the feeling the horses were talking to themselves while they were doing their thing out there, like Dirty Harry talking to a punk he is beating up on:

"You (straight out of the chute. stopping 4-legged from 10 feet in the air) measly excuse for a cowboy (sunfish right followed by whiplash left), you think you're going to ride *me*? Why, I'm gonna, and then I'm gonna, and…" (exit cowboy, stage left)… "I'm laughing at you, metrosexual!" (Well, not that last part. I made that up.)

As usual, I had not read the fine print. After the last bucking horse of the day was sold, the announcer mentioned, "Folks, make sure ya stick around fer tha Wild Horse Race." You got that right, I thought to my self…a wild horse race? I'm not going to miss anything about it.

Here's the deal: you take six wild horses, put halters on them, put them in the chutes, get six teams of three cowboys each in the middle of the arena, turn the wild horses loose, and the first cowboy to ride his wild horse all the way around the half-mile track wins. Simple, right? Wrong. Focus on the title for a minute…Wild Horse Race. Maybe I should underline that "wild" part. These horses have never seen any thing in pants until right now, and they are not impressed.

You know how this is supposed to work, but let me tell you what really happens. At a signal, they turn all six horses loose at once; what happens next is chaos. These horses come out of the chute with no intention of getting caught, so the next few minutes are spent watching three grown cowboys hanging on a lead rope while they are being drug back and forth across the arena. Since all six horses are crisscrossing the arena at the same time, things may seem to be going your way, but then another bronc gallops smack into you, with his team attached firmly to his lead rope, and it's back to square one for all concerned.

Once everybody works up a little sweat, the cowboys finally get close enough to their prey, and start putting the saddle on board. Occasionally, one of the broncs will slip and fall to his side in the dirt. Now, at the horse activities I go to, this would prompt frantic calls for the veterinary rescue squad, and so on. Not these boys. As a steed goes down on his side, you can almost hear them think "sweet." They pounce on him, the saddle is positioned, and when the bronc resurfaces, he has a brand-new appendage, and a bad attitude.

Everybody is getting a little winded at this point, including the audience, which has been laughing fit to be tied for about five minutes. Some of these broncs are serious buckers, and the cowboy has to remount several times before he can get a semblance of control. One lanky kid was thrown by a hammerheaded paint horse six times by actual count. He never did get that rascal to gallop around the track, and the last time he got bucked off, he just crawled to the edge of the arena and threw up, overcome by either exertion or Coors, or both.

The first cowboy to get his horse galloping around the track made the dangerous mistake of thinking he had things going his way. In an instant his horse had swapped ends and was headed back to the arena at a high lope. Some timely intervention by the outriders, and the addition of a couple more of the broncs on their way around the track got things going counterclockwise again.

By now the crowd was starting to really get into it, so a wall of applause and cheering greeted the prospective winner as he approached the finish line. Having just jumped off a turnip truck this morning, the horse had never been exposed to anything like this, so he naturally boogered, turned left, and jumped through the infield fence. This was not in the script. Understandably, the rest of the field of wild horses said "Hmmm, danger ahead" and either swapped ends and started back clockwise, or followed the first miscreant into the infield. The outriders had their hands full, but finally herded the survivors across the finish line. The applause set off the remaining broncs, but by this time they were too tired to put up much of a fuss, and the race was declared officially over.

There is no way to accurately describe a wild horse race, because there are as many hysterical, chaotic, funny, dangerous scenes as there are horses being turned loose. Plus, they interact in unpredictable ways...when you threw your leg over your horse, you don't plan on some other cowboy and bronc T-boning you just as you get a grip on your situation, leveling all the participants, and sending two horses, and six cowboys into a vicious, swearing, sweaty, hairball snarl of horse and humanity. It would take several video cameras to capture it all, and even then, you would have to watch it several times, because you would get to laughing so hard, you would still miss stuff.

Throughout the day, the chatter among the railbirds is rough, and humorous, and typically Western. If a rider hits the ground hard, but bounces right up again, he is not described as durable, he is "toughern' uh two-dollar steak."

The ratio between cowboys and cowgirls is about even, and there is a fair amount of sizing-up going on by both sexes.

One cowgirl to another: "Oh mah Gawd, do yah think that's a snuff can in his jeans, or a condom?"

One cowboy to his sidekick: "Now ain't she drop daid purty?" And later on, delivered in a worshipful tone, "Yah got ta love tha Lord, fur makin' sum'in' lak that!" On the other hand, one railbird observed, "Whal, if the Lord hates ugly, she ain't going to Heaven."

I had to think about it for a minute, when I overheard a cowboy state that he was "goin' ta th' street dance tonight, en fine me uh babelicious belt buckle polisher." Oh, yeah, I haven't told you about the street dance yet, have I? Both Friday and Saturday nights, Miles City hosts a street dance on Main Street, and about 10,000 people turn out. There are several country-and-western bands playing, along with a DJ, so the crowd never really slows down. The bands take turns, which causes a continual milling around, according to which street corner is happening at any particular time.

The city fathers fence off the downtown area for the street dance, and "suspend the open container laws." This is a euphemism for ignoring public drunkenness. The cops here are pretty relaxed. There are enough of them around to handle pretty much anything short of a full-scale riot. Mace and a ninja stick are real equalizers, anyway. So drunks, fools, and assorted other types of cowboys and cowgirls pretty much get a free pass. I never saw a fight, and did not notice any obvious hookers around. I suppose they wouldn't be able to stand the competition from the amateurs. Having said all that, there is such a general air of fun and amusement that you are never worried about being in the middle of a loud, rowdy crowd. The obvious police presence has something to do with it, but there are families here, from toddlers to geezers, and every one is here to have a good time. Mardi Gras in a Stetson.

The street dance bands know their clientele pretty well. You aren't going to hear a lot of Cole Porter here, but you will see some fancy two-stepping. I guess you have got to step pretty lively, if you and your partner are both wearing jeans, fancy rowel spurs, and a Stetson about a quarter acre wide. Midway through the night, we ran into my fishing buddy Pete Howell and his new girlfriend, Brooke. We said our howdys, agreed we would meet for breakfast, and left them to the dance floor. Just so you know, Pete is 6'2" and maybe 140 pounds with water in his boots...nothing but length and a grin. Tall? He could go goose hunting with a rake! Shortly after we left, Pete got a little exuberant during a fancy twirl, and clocked Brook in the middle of her forehead with his elbow. Lights out. The boy will be paying for that stunt for a long time to come, don't ya know. Blame it on a combination of Coors and the music selection. Where else could you hear such classics as:

"Bubba Shot the Jukebox Last Night"

Then there is:

"He Put the Bottle to His Head and Pulled the Trigger"
Or that perennial favorite:
"She Thinks My Tractor's Sexy"
And then of course my personal favorite:
"Drop-kick Me, Jesus, Through the Goal Posts of Life"
(I know you don't believe me...look it up.)

Anyway, I pointed out to the rest of the group that I was like the monkey making love to the porcupine; I didn't know how much more of this fun I could stand. The Coors was starting to kick in for this crowd, and somebody was fixing to have a Paris Hilton moment pretty quick. We've got another day of this, we agreed, and headed back for the KOA Kampground.

SATURDAY, MAY 21, 2005

You never know what you are going to see when you come to a bucking horse sale. Due to my jetlag, I was up early, and got to watch a grizzled cowboy walk his two border collies behind the Kampgrounds. I was a little foggy, so it took a minute for me to figure out that he had both dogs on those retractable leashes. "Cowboys have sure gone sissy on me," I thought. "Wonder what they will stoop to next?" You guessed it. As the dogs finished their constitutionals, this cowboy reached down with an inverted Ziploc bag over his hand, picked up the Tootsie Rolls as neat as you please, and disposed of the evidence in an approved container. Couldn't have done it better on Park Avenue.

Just as I was about to give up in disgust, my faith in the essential insanity of cowboys was restored by a 20-something kid who was camped out two spots down from us. He sat down outside his tent wearing nothing but boxer shorts, a 20-gallon Stetson, some Tony Llamas, and a smile, pulled out a guitar, and proceeded to serenade the sun rise. "That's more like it," I thought. "Too bad he can't sing."

Miles City doesn't want you to get bored while you wait for the sales to open, so Saturday morning they schedule a parade down Main Street. There is no theme, really, just a stream of floats, marching high school bands, civic groups, restored military vehicles, horse-drawn carriages, antique cars, tractors, the local Shriners doing a drill routine on mopeds, and the occasional late-model car, driving sedately down the center line, with a "For Sale" sign in the side window. You gotta love it.

Lunch is put on in the city park by the local Chamber of Commerce—all the BarBQ you can eat, potato salad, coleslaw, and iced tea for $5.00. If you walk away from this set-up still hungry, you are not trying. While you are eating, you can wander around and watch what they call the "quick draw." It's not what you think, but rather a group of artists who are given 30 minutes to draw/sculpt/paint something. At the end of the time period, the results are auctioned off and the proceeds go to local charities. Fun to watch.

But the crowd had come for the bucking horses, so we all wandered that way, and settled in for an afternoon of fun. This time, in addition to the bucking horses, there was Quarter Horse racing on the track, with pari-mutual betting on closed-circuit TV. The bucking horses were getting up to their usual stunts, and the racing is pretty interesting for someone used to watching Thoroughbred races. The reason they call it Quarter Horse racing is because, well, they race for a quarter mile. At the speeds they go, if you sneeze you can miss the whole thing.

The grandstand is right down on the track, so the impression of speed is overwhelming. One jockey's luck ran out right in front of us. His saddle turned and he fell off under his horse, bringing it down along with a couple of other horses and their riders. Everyone seemed fine, except for the unfortunate jockey who started it all...he hadn't moved yet. While some railbirds gathered around him, the high, metal track rail fencing at both ends of the grandstand were swung back across the track to enclose the area in front of the us, and the rodeo arena was back in business.

"Folks, we'll have tha EMTs take a look at Pablo, en' git back to ya 'bout 'im, but rat now, we got uh bucking horse to sell to ya, comin' outta chute number six." And away we went. They don't take any prisoners in Miles City. Pablo was carried out on an old door, waving his good hand at the crowd and the sales continued.

By now, the crowd had consumed more Coors than you might think possible, and had settled into a boozy, cheerful acceptance of the danger and carnage that was taking place out in front of us. The general attitude was that this was just life its own self, and besides, there was another wild horse race coming up. The sales had declined in interest for most of the crowd, but nobody was going to miss the finale. They were here for the duration.

When the wild horse race was finally announced, there was a general feeling of "all right" from the crowd, and we all stood up, so as not to miss anything. On the one hand, if you've seen one wild horse race, you've seen them all. On the other hand, for sheer energy, spectacle, and excitement, nothing beats it. Once the whistle blows and the six gates are swung open and the wild horses burst into the arena, you are transfixed.

The general alcoholic intake had red-lined by now, which contributed greatly to the inefficiency of the proceedings. It is hard to drag a wild horse to a standstill when you are feeling loppy-legged yourself. "Cowboys everywhere, fighting, swearing, struggling, intent on enforcing their will on a creature of nature," I thought, "a perfect metaphor for the opening of the West...done in a hurry by young men not in full possession of their senses, violent, crude, and wasteful of the natural resources and the wild animals that were unfortunate enough to get in their way." But my poetic ruminations did not last longer than it took for yet another bronc to flip over backwards and for several cowboys to pounce on him while the rider extricated himself, and jumped back into the fray.

Before long, a steel grey headed counterclockwise around the track, with his rider giving him a rope-a-dope with the long cotton lead shank every time the grey thought of slowing down to buck, or spin back towards the herd. Rounding the far turn, the bronc spotted his remaining compatriots, who were still engaged in bucking their riders off, running into their pals, falling down, jumping up, crashing into the fence, and generally exhibiting an uncooperative attitude. The grey put on a burst of speed towards the finish line, and his cowboy commenced to ride a powerful stretch drive, egged on by the scent of victory, and the cheers of the crowd.

Galloping back into the enclosure in front of the stands, he suddenly realized that his horse had not slackened his pace, and was headed straight towards the six-foot metal fence that by now had been pulled across the track. He pulled back on the lead rope, but there was nothing at the end of the rope but eights and aces, a dead man's hand. The grey saw the fence at the last second, but it was too late for him to stop. He twisted his neck to the left, fell to his side, and crashed into the fence sideways, slamming his rider violently against the fence and pinning him there. The horse scrambled to his feet but the cowboy did not move.

There was so much turmoil in the arena that most of the crowd missed the wreck, and it took frantic action on the part of some railbirds to get the attention of the EMTs. The announcer was still unaware, thanking the crowd for coming, and reminding us to drive safely on the way home. We followed the stream of people towards the exit, which led us past the scene where the cowboy lay, crumpled and still. A young cowboy, obviously a friend, leaned over one of the EMTs, and asked a question. Moving with the disciplined haste of the well-trained, the EMT, grim faced, merely shook his head in reply. The friend, black hat, blue jeans, purple-and-black striped shirt, bent over, picked up his friends' hat, absent mindedly knocked the dust off it, straightened up, and looked off towards the Badlands. The look on his face, the grief of the helpless, was all you had to know. I wanted to say something to him, but there was nothing to say. Underneath the noise of a drunken crowd on the move, I could hear Toby Keith's refrain: "...the best you can hope for is to die with your boots on."

I took one more look over my shoulder, then followed the rest of the crowd out of the gate, and turned East.

GREETINGS FROM SYDNEY*

In the spring of 2000, Primedia got in touch with me, and asked if I would write a series of articles about the Olympics in Sydney for Equisearch. Equisearch is what kids these days refer to as a "zine," meaning a virtual web magazine. Gail and I had been talking about going down to watch, and this was the excuse we needed.

Before you read these reports from the 2000 Olympics, let me tell you a story. I went "down under" with what I would like to think is a classical journalist's attitude; tell the reader who, what, where, and I forget the others. There are only three kinds of people—those that can count, and those that can't. Anyway, where was I? Oh, yeah, in Sydney. Any way, you will notice that the first day's report is pretty cut

*Permission to reprint by EquiSearch.com

and dried, for me. "So-and-so is in first with a score of such-and-such," and like that. However, a strange thing happened before I wrote the second day's article. I went back to the motel room with my notes and results. I happened to check my email before I started writing.

When I got my email opened up, there was a message from a knowledgeable friend, asking about the reason behind someone's score from earlier that day. I remember pushing back from the desk and thinking "Wow, he's not asking about the scores from yesterday, he's asking about today's scores. He was watching the same event I was, on the Internet!"

I suddenly realized the power of the Internet. All my plans for the article I was going to write were badly out of date, because the world had already found out the scores, and knew the placings. If I was going to keep people interested in the articles, it would be because of my commentary, not my reportage. It is amusing to me now to reread these articles and watch as I struggle to change my point of view. But I had a lot of fun doing that, and I hope that comes through in these articles.

SEPTEMBER 15, 2000

Greetings from Sydney. I am going to pass along my personal reactions and experiences from the Olympics here in Australia. Don't expect them to be complete, or even accurate, but I hope you do find them interesting, and entertaining.

First things first. All eight of our horses, both Team and Individual, passed the first veterinary exam today. If you think event riders get nervous before cross-country, you should see them at the veterinary examinations. Riders hate this process, because there is nothing they can do to influence the outcome. So there are plenty of long faces around before they jog, and plenty of smiles after.

It is amazing how the horses show their personality at the "jog." Giltedge, Prince Panache, and Custom Made, all consummate pros. They walked in, ears up, strutted up and down the lane and walked out, flat footed. They know the routine, and they weren't too fussed: "Just another Olympics, boss."

Anderoo and Chevalier, both with a bloom on their coats to die for, trotting with all four feet off the ground at once. Hogan's Hero and Hyde Park Corner, rolling their eyes at the sizable, and knowledgeable, crowd gathered to watch. They both looked like mules going up a ladder going away from the judges, and both took their jockeys for a ride on the way home, obviously in peak condition.

The most humorous moment of the day was Nina Fout, warning the ring stewards that 3 Magic Beans could be a little dangerous to be around when he gets excited. "Yeargh, nah worries, Sheila," said one bushie (as red necks are known down here), just before diving over a crowd control barrier, a microsecond ahead of a pair of hooves. Nina is second to go for the team on Saturday afternoon, and I imagine she will skip the opening ceremonies, so as to be in the saddle early and often on Saturday.

You wonder about these kids. They want to fly halfway around the world to jump over obstacles that no one has ever seen before, on ground that no one has galloped on, and they can't wait. An obviously elated Linden Wiesman, bouncing on her toes with a slightly maniac grin on her face, summed it up for her teammates. "I'm ready," she said. You wonder about these kids, but you gotta love 'em.

David O'Connor will captain our team this year. He is an unusual mix of intellect and intuition, and was destined for Olympic medals at an early age. Not many people these days can say that they have ridden across the United States on horseback. Even fewer can say they did it at age 12. No wonder he sits so well in dressage now, he burned off the nerve endings on his seat bones long ago.

Giltedge is a reliable performer at this level, and that must have been a factor in the selector's thinking, when they started looking at the list of horses and riders who have no prior Olympic experience. When you are building a team, it is a great comfort to know you have a horse that can finish with a final score under 50. Earlier this year, I asked Mark Phillips, the USET coach, if a final team score of 150 would be good enough for a gold medal. "I should think it will need to be lower than that," he replied. (Remember, the top three scores count.)

We can count on David for that sort of performance, as his horses have been training well, and just as important, David is as healthy as he has been in years. He has been plagued by shoulder and rib injuries since '97; and I think we will see a fitter, more athletic ride from him, and that has to be good news for us.

Jack LeGoff, the most successful Event trainer of all time, once remarked that it is as hard to get four sound riders to the Games as it is to get four sound horses there. If you don't believe him, just ask Rodney Powell. He was named to the British team, but broke his ankle while walking his Olympic mount through Horsley Park, thus ending his Olympic bid. Walking!

Certainly, Karen O'Connor is no stranger to the risks of the sport, having had her share of mental and physical ups and downs over the last 25 years. But she could not have a better friend to ride during what will almost certainly be her last Olympic effort. Prince Panache is a lovely, dark brown thoroughbred. The description that comes to mind is "genuine." I think the only thing in the world he is afraid of is that he will not do his best. There aren't many like him around, and we can thank our lucky stars that he came into the hands of such a superlative horsewoman.

Prince Panache is too big for Karen, at 17 hands, and he is too old, at 16. Fortunately, no one has told Karen or "Nache." They have had a good training camp, are both veterans, and both know that; for them, the future is now. On a good day they can finish in the high 30s.

Joining the two O'Connors on the Team of four riders are Nina Fout on her own 3 Magic Beans, and Linden Wiesman on Barbara and Jim Wiesman's Anderoo. There must be something in the water around Middleburg, Virginia, as all four riders live within 10 miles of each other.

Eventing is a lonely discipline...riders spend years to develop their skills, they wait until there is a Three-Day Event for them to showcase their skills, and then wait even more years for the right horse to come along. But not many have waited as long, or worked as hard for so little to show for it, as Nina Fout. Her

Olympic dreams started over 20 years ago, with her first trip to the North American Young Rider Championships.

A resounding win in the prestigious Peters Trophy at the Radnor Three-Day Event in 1975 made her the Junior National Champion, and showed the horse world what she could do. But over the years, she has had the most incredible string of injuries to her horses and herself. A crashing fall at the same event several years later sidelined her for six months, with serious head and neck injuries. Horses that looked promising turned out to lack the desire, or the scope, or that mysterious quality that makes one horse just a horse, and another horse that rarest of all equines, an Olympic horse.

But throughout all those years, one thing never changed. Nina never gave up on herself, and she never let go of her dream. So here she is. And if you ever dream of riding in the Olympics, dream of 3 Magic Beans. He is a thoroughbred, and he looks like one. He is light on his feet, fast, fearless, and has the "look of eagles." Over the past three years, Nina and "Beans" have jumped clean over the biggest courses in the world: Badminton, Burghley, and Kentucky.

It is a great source of confidence to a rider to know, rather than think, your horse can do it. And Nina knows that her greatest challenge will occur not on the cross-country course, but in the Dressage arena. Beans is nothing if not competitive, and the bigger the occasion the more competitive he becomes. Nina will be sitting on a powder keg, and it is going to take every ounce of her skill to prevent the explosion. If she can get a quiet ride out of him in the Dressage ring, the rest of the week will seem easy to her. An Olympic cross-country course can be Kryptonite to some horses. Beans will think it is catnip.

At 25, Linden Wiesman is the youngest member of the team, but she has the same strange, almost surreal self-confidence that her teammates display. It is a given that athletes at this level are self-confident, and part of our fascination with the Olympics is to see how well humans can perform under incredible pressure. Linden's attitude does not come across as, "I'm better than you," but rather, "If I get my chance, I know what I can do."

Like Nina Fout, Linden is a former Junior National Champion. But for a while it did not look as if she would ever get her chance at the Olympics. First one horse, then another, would get hurt, lose desire, or lack the power for the massive obstacles that an Olympic horse will need. Then, just as things started to come around for her, Linden had a series of injuries that would have permanently grounded a normal person. But if you can shrug off a broken pelvis, followed by a broken femur (the big bone above the knee), then Linden shrugged them off.

Top-class athletes are quick healers, and Linden was no exception. She was back in the saddle much sooner than the experts predicted, and training as hard as ever. When her lesson was over, Linden would jump down from the saddle with the rest of the students. But when she thought no one was looking, getting down from the saddle was a long, slow, painful attempt to ease an obviously damaged body gently to the ground. I was Linden's coach during this period, and the only reason I did not take her out of training was my respect for the sheer courage and desire to excel that I saw her display. It is hard to bench an athlete who won't give up.

At the same time, Linden had finally developed a horse that had the necessary qualities. Anderoo is a 10-year-old, bay, thoroughbred gelding. He is a classy, breedy looking creature, with large luminous eyes, that seem to gaze at the far horizon in search of fields to gallop over. Of course, with an attitude like this he is a quirky fellow to ride, especially in the Dressage.

Over fences, he does not take well to being hand ridden, and it took a while for Linden to find out that she had to literally trust him with her life. It is a terrifying sensation for a good rider, to be galloping at a big fence, waiting until the horse decides where to take off. It has not all been plain sailing for her, and I do not think many riders would have had the skill, patience and intuition that it took to get Anderoo to the Olympics. But Linden did, and here they are, ready to ride down the centerline with the U.S.A. flag on their saddlecloth.

If Linden can score lower than 55 in the dressage, and if Nina can break 60, you will see a thin sheen of sweat break out on the Kiwi's, Aussie's, and Brit's foreheads.

In a funny way, Karen and David's, and all of our Olympic hopes for a Gold medal rest squarely in the hands of two horse-women who have never ridden at the Olympic level before. We know what Karen and David can do...they have done it before. So all the work and struggle and money and time and injury and success and disappointment, all this comes down on the shoulders of two rookies from Virginia. The selectors hope they are ready. I think they are ready. Nina and Linden know they are.

SEPTEMBER 16, 2000

Greetings from Sydney. After the first two riders on each team completed the Dressage phase today, the Australian team has a commanding lead. Andrew Hoy, on the gorgeous grey, Darien Powers, has a score of 30.6 to lead the way. Hoy showed his years of experience when he came into the arena in front of a highly partisan and vocal crowd, and held his finger to his lips, asking for quiet. He then proceeded to ride a personal best, and pumped both fists in the air as he left the arena. Needless to say, the crowd roared its approval.

Hoy's American-based fellow countryman, Phillip Dutton, on House Doctor, scored 46.6, to give the Australian team a first day total of 77.2. The British team is a not-so-close second, with 94.6, followed by the French at 98.6, and the U.S., at 103.0. The only surprise of the day was the New Zealand team, finishing with 109.6. Two-time Gold medalist Mark Todd scored a disappointing 58.6, on an obviously agitated Diamond Hall Red.

David O'Connor got the U.S. contingent off to a great start with a score of 44.4. He certainly knows his horse...the judge rang the bell, the crowd hushed and settled back in their seats, in expectation of another patented O'Connor performance...and David halted 10 yards from the entrance, dropped the reins, and patted Giltedge on the neck. He calmly waited while Giltedge rubbed his nose on his foreleg, picked up the reins, cantered a circle and entered the arena as if nothing had happened. The look on Mark Phillips' face while all this was going on was special.

But the score made it all worthwhile, and David had the third best performance of the day, just four tenths of a point behind Lesley Law, of Great Britain, on Shear H2O. It says something about David's skill level in this phase, when U.S. supporters are slightly disappointed that he is not in first place after dressage.

In 1984 at the Los Angeles Olympics, Virginia Holgate from Great Britain said, "When I rode down the center line, I have never felt such a sense of occasion." (This from a winner of European Championships, Badminton, Burghley, etc.) I imagine that when Nina Fout aimed 3 Magic Beans at the center line this afternoon, she was thinking, "I wonder if I can keep the lid on him for seven minutes?" The answer is that not only did she keep the lid on, she scored a 58.6. You have to be fairly pleased with yourself, when you get the same score as Mark Todd.

This was a big, big, BIG performance from Nina. Now her next two teammates, Linden Wiesman and Karen O'Connor don't have to play catch up. In Eventing, team work is a funny thing. You don't pass a baton for this team, but you can do something even harder, and more important. You can take the pressure off your teammates, just by doing your job. And when doing your job means going to the Olympics as a rookie, and riding the best dressage test you have ever ridden, your teammates catch fire. (Seasoned coaches know this...why do you think Olympic veterans such as Mark Todd, Andrew Hoy, and David O'Connor are going first for their teams?)

So look for some good scores from Linden and Karen tomorrow. Linden won't win it, but she has been improving daily; and if the judges show up in a good mood, she could easily score under 55; and from the look on Karen's face the last couple of days, she feels that she can go for it. If I were a betting man, I would not bet against a score in the low 30s for Karen and Nache. The Australians have the lead, but it is not insurmountable, there is a long way to go, and we have as good a chance as anybody.

I went to my first Olympic Games in London in 1948, and I've watched a few since then. One of the most interesting things about that time was the way one could identify riders' nationality by the way they rode. The Germans were always upright in the saddle, while the Italians were crouched up their horse's neck, and so on. That is a thing of the past. All these riders sit well these days, and they all look more or less the same, which is to say fabulous.

Back in the States, the real fans are going to be going over the scores and saying, "Are those judges smoking something stronger than cigarettes?" The average score today was about 15 points better than it would be at Kentucky, Badminton, or Burghley. That is not a function of bad judging, but of really good riding. The standard is very high, and we are seeing the results of it. These riders sit like Kings and Queens, their horses are on the bit, and they are really moving. There was been a refreshing lack of caution in the ring today. These riders have been training for a long time, and they are ready to show it off to the crowd.

And that's another thing. This crowd knows what it is watching. Little murmurs of appreciation or dismay run through the crowd as each horse and rider perform. The crowd has come from all over the world because they love horses, and they are getting their money's worth.

It is hard to just watch the horses, when the people watching is at such a premium. What would you give to listen to General Jack Burton, Sally O'Connor, and Captain Jack Fritz (all International judges) comment on the scores? Or watch Hamish Lachore, the organizer of the Burgie Horse Trials in Scotland, in the middle of the Japanese contingent, chatting away. Talk about two people separated by a common language. At least he wasn't wearing a skirt.

"Let the Games begin!" Are you kidding? The only games around here are being played at "Panthers," the casino nearby. These Olympics are about as professional as you can get. You may have noticed a lack of direct quotes in my comments. That is because if a reporter is not accredited, the athlete is not allowed to talk to them on the record. The quotes are reserved for the sponsors; I mean major media, i.e., NBC and accredited press. It gives new meaning to the old line about money talks.

But the Aussies are trying to do things right. Got a transport problem the day before the opening ceremonies? Just have the Australian government call out the army, for extra bus drivers.

Got clay soil at the proposed site for the equestrian venue? No worries, mate, just grade a five-mile long track, bring in sand and shavings, seed it, and then water and mow it for three years.

Americans feel at home here in Australia, where there is a breezy informality. The Aussies are laid back without being lazy, and are having a grand time showing their country off. They are big sports fans down under, and every Australian rider who comes in to the ring does so to the accompaniment of this strange Antipodean war-cry..."aussie, ausSIE, AUSSIE!" If you hold your nose, and think "ollie, ollie oxen free" with a rising inflection, you will get a pretty good approximation of it, just 20,000 times louder.

Sydney obviously has a no-high-rise policy. There are no tall buildings outside of downtown, which lends a very human, livable feel to the area. The architecture is a strange mixture...English cottages, with red tile roofs...sort of San Diego with tea and a twang.

Eventing has its moments, but the real risk sport around here is ducking the kangaroos on the roads after dark. The USET's Jim Wolf has already had one kangaroo "kamikaze" his rent-a-car, and the story goes that another team got a little too much Foster's lager in it's eye, hit a 'roo with their car, thought it needed medical attention, threw a jacket (with an athlete's credentials in the pocket) over it, and turned around to see the 'roo, and the jacket, bounding into the bush. Sort of a down under version of the dog ate my homework.

SEPTEMBER 17, 2000

Greetings from Sydney. Strong performances by a newcomer and an Olympic veteran moved the U.S. team into third place after the conclusion of two days of dressage. The Australian team total of 112.6 keeps them in first place, followed by Great Britain with 115.2, and the U.S. with 125.4.

How close is the competition? If one Australian does not go clear on the cross-country course, and the other teams are error free, it could drop the Aussies into fourth place. I saw Andrew Hoy, the Aussie team captain and best placed rider to date, after the scores were posted and he looked like a man with a lot on his mind. Remember Butch Cassidy and the Sundance Kid, watching the posse chasing them? "Where do they get these guys?" That's Andrew.

The second day of dressage started at 9:30 a.m., and by 10:00 two riders had posted scores in the low 30s. Pippa Funnel of G.B. got a well-deserved 32.0 on the powerful and elegant Supreme Rock, and the Australian rider, Stuart Tinney, lit up the stadium with Jeepster, with a score of 36.0. Jeepster was obviously fit and on the edge throughout the performance, but Stuart gave him a tactful ride, while the crowd held its breath. As he turned down the center line for the final time to finish his test, international dressage judge Sally O'Connor murmured, "This place is going to erupt." She was right. It did.

Later in the day Great Britain's Ian Stark, on Jaybee, got a 39.2, and Germany's Ingrid Klimke, daughter of the legendary dressage Gold medalist Reiner Klimke, showed that she knows a thing or two about it as well, with a score of 36.2.

The U.S. supporters had come to see how our mixed team of veterans and newcomers would measure up against the best in the world. Was this the best team we could field, or had the selectors missed something?

As it turned out, the only thing missing from Linden Wiesman's dressage test today was a halo. Her score of 48.4 is already the best she and Anderoo have ever done. Then take in to account that she is a rookie. Traditionally judges do not give rookies the marks they deserve, so you see why experienced observers who watched her test felt she should have scored at least five marks better. But that is part of the game at the Games, and Linden just smiled and shrugged when her score was announced. Hopefully, in 20 years at some other Olympic Games, she will get the benefit of the halo effect. But for now her supporters, while mildly disappointed with her score, are elated with her performance.

So the stage was set for Prince Panache and Karen O'Connor, the final combination for the U.S. An average ride wasn't going to get it done for the team. There had been too many superlative performances by other nations. Only something extraordinary from Karen and Nache would do. And so Karen and her gallant giant, as they have so many times over the years, turned in the performance the team absolutely, positively had to have. And what a performance! Her score of 32.6 was good enough to move the team into third, only 12.8 behind the Australians.

There are 21 marks given in this test, from 0 to 10. There are three judges, so that makes 63 total marks. Karen's lowest mark, her *lowest* mark, was a 7. Most riders would kill for a 7. But one of the hallmarks of a champion is consistency, so there you have it.

I cannot remember ever seeing a team go to the Olympics and have all four riders score a personal best. Horses just don't work that way. But here we are, in third place after the first phase of competition, with a real chance at winning. I don't know who I am prouder of...Karen and David did what superstars are supposed to do (that's why they are superstars). Nina and Linden stepped out onto the world stage for the first time, and only rode better than they ever have in their entire lives. No one knows what is going to happen tomorrow, but so far, so good.

Before the real fun starts tomorrow, I want to tell you a little about the cross-country course. The course designer, Mike Etherington-Smith, has a problem. He has to test the best without eliminating the rest. So he has designed a course with that in mind. When you leave the start box on this course, you had better bring your brain along. This thing is big *and* technical. That's the way it is supposed to be at the Olympics, and that's the way this one is. The first thing I noticed about the course is that there is a lot of rise and fall in the terrain. This means that whatever you build will ride just that little bit harder, and be just that little bit more tiring for the horses.

The first part of the course tends uphill, and Mike has given the riders a few simple fences to get into their rhythm, if you consider 3'11" by 5'9"simple. I've seen condominiums smaller than these things. Probably the first problems will occur at 7a & b, the Boorooborongal Brushes. These are two ditch-and-hedges, set about 100 degrees from each other. It will take a brave horse, to jump on an extreme angle over 7a, take two strides uphill to 7b, and jump again. If your horse tends to swerve either way, you will be better off to jump them as separate obstacles. The time lost turning right handed downhill and then coming straight back uphill to the second element is no match for 20 penalties for a refusal.

After a simple "fly" fence (that means you should jump it on the fly), there is a long downhill run to the first water jump at 10 and 11abc. There is an evil, symbiotic relationship between crowds, water jumps, and course designers. Water is always a problem for horses, because they never know how deep the water is before they jump into it. Course designers know this, so they tend to build something special here. Crowds know they will see something special at the water jump, so Pemulwy's Waterhole will draw the biggest crowd on the first half of the course.

I don't think they will be disappointed here. Picture a massive log, set about 3'7" high, followed 12 feet later by an identical log, that has a 6' drop behind it, landing in 9" of water. You then take four or five strides and jump a corner, taking off and landing again in the water.

Remember the part where I said the riders had to take their brain along? This is what I was talking about. If your horse lands short and weak, you had better take five strides. If you land long and strong in the water, you had better kick for four strides. Either option will work...but if you land and just sit there, fat, dumb, and happy, then you will get to the corner at 11c on a half-stride, and there's no hope for you...you will have a refusal.

There is a long way around the complex, but it is really long, and the first few riders will be testing their luck here. This combination is very similar to the second water jump at Kentucky CCI**** three years ago, and most of the riders think that while this one is bigger, it is doable.

There is a long gallop to settle you into a rhythm again, then another complex, the Abbotsbury Farmyard, 13abcd. Again there is a long way around the farmyard, but most of the riders will jump two right-handed corners, with two strides in between. It is easy, once you know how.

After a long down hill run (the first on the course), you come to the second water jump. The Devil's Back Billabong, 15abcde, is a big log with a drop in to water, four strides to an up-bank, bounce over a log back into water, four strides across the water, up a slope and out over a ditch-and-hedge. Oh, did I mention that the ditch-and-hedge is a little narrow, right where you want to jump it?

Whenever you see that many letters after a number, it means Mike Etherington-Smith has been burning the midnight oil again. Of course, there is a long way around, but it will take forever, and by this time, you might as well keep coming on a straight line. When you land after this little exercise, you need to listen to your horse, as you have done a lot of jumping, and he may need a breather. If he is OK, away you go, but if he needs to catch his breath, this is the place to do it.

The next few fences are big, but designed to be ridden at the gallop. So the next problem fences are 22 and 23abc, the Orphan School Seats. You and I would call this combination a sunken road, and indeed it is based on the sunken road complex at Kentucky. This would be a hard jump anywhere, but it is extra hard at this point in the course.

You jump a chair, take a stride, drop down into a sunken road, take a stride there, jump up a bank the same size, take two strides, and jump another chair at quite an angle. The technical part here is that horses tend to jump too big jumping down, and they tend to wander when you jump up. So you have to have them under control, which is hard to do, considering all the downhill galloping you have just done. That's why you do all that dressage, so that they will still listen to you when they get their blood up. You have to get it right here...too slow, and you will have a refusal going in...too fast and you will miss the last part of 23c. If it was easy, everyone would do it, right? The alternate route here is safe, but once again very slow.

There is no letup now, because 24 and 25, the Providence Haysheds, pose the same question as 23, but on the other side. The danger at the Orphan School Seats is that you can run past them to the right. Here at 24 and 25, the danger is that you may run left past the second of the two houses. The angle here is acute, but possible, with one stride in between. Think Badminton's Luckington Lane with a green tin roof and you've got it.

The final problems will probably occur at 28ab, Vinegar Hill. This is very similar to the Quarrys at Badminton and Kentucky, with a big drop going in and a bending line to a narrow fence at the top of the hill coming out. It isn't anything you haven't seen before, but it is big, and late in the course.

Then it is quite a long climb up hill over big, but simple fences, to the last fence, 32, The Hellenic Omega.

It is a hard course overall, but very fair, and very jumpable. So the competition will be won not just by the jumping, but by speed. I am going to stick my neck out and predict that between five and seven horses will make the time to finish with their dressage scores. If a couple of those horses are ours, we will definitely move up in the placings.

SEPTEMBER 18, 2000

Greetings from Sydney. The Australian team maintained their lead after the cross-country phase of the Olympics, with an over night score of 114.2. Great Britain is close on the Aussie's heels, with 127.0, and New Zealand moved up from 5th to 3rd, with a two-day total of 151.2. Falls and time faults moved the U.S. team down to 4th place, with a score of 160.8.

On a picture-perfect day, 55,000 spectators watched as four Australian riders turned in rides of near perfection. All four jumped clean, and had a grand total of five seconds over the time. That's five seconds total, spread over the nearly 20 miles of cross-country course that these riders covered today. Andrew Hoy set the tone for the Aussies with a smooth, flowing round, and finished with his dressage score of 30.6. His teammates soon followed, and when they had all finished, it was clear that Australia was poised to win a record-breaking third consecutive gold medal.

When asked about his team, Australian Chef d'Equipe, Wayne Roycroft said, "I'm really pleased with our program. We have about 60 riders riding regularly at the upper levels, and our old fellows really had to work to make the team this time." The thought of another 60 Andrew Hoys is enough to make other coaches pull their hair.

The Brits did not hang around today, either. They had three clean and fast rounds, and their record was not affected by Ian Stark's somewhat sketchy round on Jaybee. The New Zealanders showed some real determination today, with three double clears by Mark Todd, Blythe Tait, and Vaughn Jefferis.

David O'Connor, on Giltedge, first to go for the U.S., was clean and just outside the time to finish with a two-day total of 46.8. Nina Fout and 3 Magic Beans set out well, but Beanie gradually got stronger and stronger, forcing her to slow down before the fences in order to avoid a fall. By the second water jump at 14, Beanie was pulling so hard that Nina lost her reins as they jumped the big bounce back into water, and had to pull off to the right hand side, thus avoiding a refusal at 15, but incurring more lost time. The course was too difficult to make up any time and the end result of all this struggle was that Nina finished with a clear round, but 20 time faults.

With two clear rounds safely home, American supporters could be forgiven a mild sense of optimism as Linden Wiesman started out. But that feeling only lasted until Anderoo slipped on the turn before the first water at 10. He recovered his balance by adding a stride, but this put him too close to the log, and he and Linden had a crashing fall. A somewhat dazed Linden speedily remounted, and continued the course.

By the Orphans School Seats, they seemed to be regaining their rhythm, but at the last instant Anderoo refused at the seat before the sunken road. At the second attempt, he jumped, but left his right knee down, and the impact caused a second fall for

Linden, and thus mandatory retirement from the course. Linden quietly remounted, and gave Anderoo a reassuring pat on the neck. She looked down the valley for an moment, as if she could see the mirage of what might have been. Then she started the long walk home, surrounded by thousands of spectators, but alone with her thoughts.

So the pressure was on Karen O'Connor and Prince Panache. If she did not jump clean and fast, the U.S.A. would have no chance for a medal. But athletes like Karen and Nache live for this sort of chance, and barring a near disaster at the Orphan School Seats, Karen turned in a fabulous round, to finish just one second over the time.

And with that effort, which was as nice a display of precision at speed as we saw all day, the U.S.A. stands just one knock down and a few time faults away from an Olympic medal.

How good was the Team competition here? So good that over a course that had the experts scratching their heads, eight riders jumped double clears (no jump faults, no time faults), and eight more riders were less than 10 seconds over the time limit. Of the top three teams best three riders, those nine riders had a combined jump penalty score of...are you ready?...(drum roll)...zero. The top nine riders were, combined, less than a minute late. Heck, several of the lower-placed riders were that late all by themselves. The Australians are such gracious winners that the rest of the horse world doesn't seem to mind that they have dominated Olympic Eventing for the past 12 years.

SEPTEMBER 19, 2000

Greetings from Sydney. The Australian Eventing team won an unprecedented third Gold medal in a row today, holding off a late challenge by the Silver medal British team, and the Bronze finishers, the United States. In front of a capacity, and highly partisan, crowd of 20,000, Australian team captain Andrew Hoy galloped through the finish line to clinch the victory. As Andrew pulled up after his round, he started to walk out, but changed his mind and rode another circle, waving at the crowd. Finally, he walked out, glancing over his shoulder at the crowd, and for an instant I could hear him think, "This moment is too perfect...I don't ever want it to end." But after a final glance around the stadium he turned his eyes forward, and left the ring. I can't remember such an explosion as greeted the Australian team on their entrance into the stadium to receive their medals. That strange Australian war cry of "aussie, ausSIE, AUSSIE!" got a real workout today

The old broadcaster's cliché, "And the crowd goes wild," had nothing on the stadium at Horsley Park. Maybe that's why I like the Aussies so much...they are happy drunks. But six hours earlier, at the final vet inspection, they did not look so happy. Andrew's horse was decidedly stiff, and an audible sigh of relief went through the crowd when the Ground Jury passed him.

The American horses all looked well and passed without further discussion by the judges. The only thing noteworthy was that 3 Magic Beans had finally gotten enough work, and stopped acting like such an idiot in front of the crowd. So it looked like our luck had turned.

But Blythe Tait, the reigning Olympic and World Champion, was not so lucky. Reddy Teddy was not level behind. A spell in the holding area did nothing for him, and he was eliminated on reinspection. This finished the New Zealanders chance for a medal, as Vaughn Jefferis had already withdrawn Bounce, and likewise Paul O'Brian with Enzed. Thus the U.S. team that had looked so far out of touch the night before was back in contention.

A clear round by David O'Connor and a clear round with five time faults by Nina Fout, set the stage for Karen O'Connor to ensure a medal for the U.S. An obviously tired Prince Panache tipped two rails, but held things together long enough to nail down the Bronze medal spot.

"I am so lucky to have a horse like him. He just brings out the best in me," said Karen. Under the old rules, her best would have been good enough for a Bronze Individual medal.

The U.S. team will return home with a Bronze medal, which ordinarily would be cause for celebration. But there is an air of unfinished business in the barn area tonight. They think they can do better the next time around. I know they can.

The Olympics always are good for memories and special moments. For example: the sign way up in the cheap seats that said simply "NZ loves you Mark." For someone like Mark Todd, who has been under intense press scrutiny for the past three months, this must have been welcome support. With his team in disarray around him, and his private life being picked over by the tabloid press, this is not the way the FEI (Federation Equestre Internationale) Horseman of the Century wanted to go into retirement.

The individual competition starts on Wednesday. I think the standard of horses and riders down here is so high that the winner will finish on their dressage score. That doesn't mean that the course is that easy, it means these guys are that good. By my calculations, David O'Connor will win the Gold for the USA, with Andrew Hoy of Australia winning the Silver, and Mary Thompson from Great Britain winning the Bronze. Look for good placings for Julie Burns and Bobby Costello. How's that for sticking your neck out?

The vet check for the individual competition was held this afternoon. I have never seen so many horses in one place at one time with such a bloom on their coats. All of our horses passed and looked really well. We have a fabulous draw, with all three horses in the final group, which always helps in the dressage phase. (The judges tend to get a little more generous as they go along.) As Bobby Costello walked in with Deirdre Pirie's Chevalier, who was meant to be her late daughter, Amanda Pirie Warrington's ride here, I had a sudden flash back to Amanda's incredible, luminous smile, and I knew she was watching.

Journalists are supposed to be objective, so I have tried to downplay my fondness for our four riders. I know I haven't done a very good job of it but I have tried. Yet the fact remains that I have a unique view of all four of them, as at one time or another, they were students of mine. So I thought I would share some impressions of them with you.

In 1994, Linden said, "I have a really cute four-year-old I want you to see." It only took one cross rail for me to fall in love with him, too. Of course that four-year-old was Anderoo, whose best...and Linden's...is yet to come.

Nina bounced at the trot dreadfully as a junior, but she would try her heart out, and I remember thinking, "If this kid doesn't give up, she is going to go somewhere." She didn't. She did.

It occurred to me on more than one occasion that I might not ever get David to focus long enough to develop his talent. Picture a younger and much more volatile Jim Wofford, with his index finger pressed into a much younger David O'Connor's chest...."Goddamn it, David, when I told you I wanted you to make your mark on the world, I did not mean for you to bush-hog your initials in my hay field!" David has written his name into the record books since then.

And Karen. I taught Karen a great deal about horses, but I learned a great deal more about words like "intrepid" and "indomitable" from her. We are so lucky to have her, and all of them. They make us proud to be horsewomen and -men, and proud to be an American.

September 20, 2000

Greetings from Sydney. When U.S. team captain David O'Connor came down to breakfast this morning, everyone asked him anxiously if he was ready to go. He replied that he was going to show the judges a "Godfather test." (For the uninitiated, that's a test the judges can't turn down.) Riding Ms. Jacquie Mars' Custom Made, his score of 29.0 put him in first place after the dressage phase, with a 5.8 point lead over Germany's Marina Koehncke. Her ride on Longchamps was good enough for a score of 34.8.

There is a truly international cast of characters rounding out the top 6 spots. Heidi Antikatzidis, riding Michaelmas is in third place for Greece with a score of 37.4, while two-time Gold medalist Mark Todd of New Zealand, riding Eyespy II is close behind her. His score of 39.0 was barely enough to hold off the challenges of three-time Australian Gold medalist Andrew Hoy, riding Swizzle In, and Sophia Andler from Sweden, on Amaretto. They are tied with equal scores of 39.8.

Several of the hot prospects looked unsettled, and did not perform as well as their riders had hoped. Ian Stark, Mary Thompson, Karen Dixon, and Blythe Tait all had subpar performances today, but Robert Costello was delighted with Chevalier's test, which has him in ninth place going into tomorrow's cross-country phase.

The cross-country course follows the same basic track as the Team competition, but course designer Michael Etherington-Smith has done a clever job of changing the fences around, and his efforts have been met with unanimous approval.

The riders all feel confident about the fences, especially since many of them have gotten their eye in during the team competition. While no one thinks the course is a pushover, there is more of a relaxed air about the individual competition, now that the pressure of riding for one's team has been lifted. All this should make for a real race against the clock tomorrow, and an exciting competition. The U.S.A. is poised for its best chance at an individual Gold medal since 1976, when Tad Coffin won at Montreal.

SEPTEMBER 21, 2000

About the only thing faster than David O'Connor's double clear on the Individual cross-country course is the speed of the Internet, spreading the good news around the world. By the time I got back to file this article, I had emails from the States, asking for more information. The basic story is this: With only the show-jumping phase left to go, the Individual Gold is David's to lose. He has an 8.4 point lead over Heidi Antikatzidis, and a 10 point lead over Mark Todd.

Toddy did not feature in many of the "likely to win" lists, which was probably just the way he wanted it. I watched him turn in another display of cool precision at high speed, and I was surprised at the strong sense of sorrow and loss I had, as he galloped over the last fence.

The sport has never seen anyone like him, and I just thank my lucky stars I was around to see him perform. I was in the twilight of my career when he started his, and after the Los Angeles Olympics, I was asked by a reporter what I thought about him." I think I retired just in time," I replied, "Toddy won't just beat you, he will embarrass you." If you thought the stadium was rocking for the team medal ceremony, wait 'til you hear the place if Toddy and Andrew Hoy get a piece of the action.

But I wouldn't count Heidi out. She is a fierce competitor, with nothing to lose and everything to gain, so the pressure won't be too severe on her. The pressure is completely off Bobby Costello and Julie Black, with their clear rounds cross-country. Bobby stands sixth tonight, only three points away from a medal, and Julie rode the round of her life to keep her somewhat green Hyde Park Corner focused from beginning to end.

And for sure, focus was the name of the game over Mike Etherington-Smith's course today. Referring to his team course, Mike said that "the boys and girls made it look easy." Maybe so, but the Individual course was no pushover.

The first rider on the course only got as far as fence 4. He adopted the toilet seat over an Olympic-sized drop, and of course came off over the shoulder. His horse wisely left town, and so it went. The likes of Andrew Hoy would go blazing past, and indeed for a moment this course would look easy. But lose your focus for a second, and your Matilda was well and truly waltzed. Many of the questions on the course were obvious questions, but you still had to have the right answers, and having the right answers for these Olympic-level questions was, well, hard.

There will be endless discussions about the relative difficulty of the two tracks. The fact remains that the good horses and riders went well, and the not so good, or good but not so lucky, went home.

But for today, the story was David O'Connor, and Custom Made. When he galloped through the finish line today, the supporter's tent erupted, but this time it went "Yankee, YanKEE, YANKEE, Oi, Oi, Oi!"

Greetings from Sydney. I never remember my dreams. I did not mention it earlier because I am so superstitious, but when I woke up yesterday morning, I remembered this dream. In my mind, I could still hear the crowd at Horsley Park, chanting "Yankee,Yankee,Yankee, Oi, Oi, Oi!" And so it was today, as David O'Connor won the Individual Gold medal, ahead of Andrew Hoy of Australia, and Mark Todd of New Zealand. David came into the ring knowing that he could knock down two fences, but then could afford to have no time faults, since Andrew was 10.8 behind in the silver medal spot.

He jumped seven fences perfectly, landed well...and started to turn the wrong way! A groan from the crowd got David's attention, and he was back on course, but you won't hear much about "blonde moments" around the O'Connor household for a while. Custom Made knocked down the ninth, to add further drama to the situation, and then galloped home inside the time for no further penalties.

"I was really worried about the seventh fence, because I thought Tailor would knock it down," said David, "and I was listening to hear if it had fallen down, and nearly missed my turn." Jay O'Connor, David's father, was heard to grumble, "I'm going to buy that boy a road map."

But none of this bothered the U.S. supporters, who made up in volume for what they lacked in numbers. As David started off on his victory gallop, the U.S. Equestrian team's Jim Wolf darted under the fence and handed David the U.S. flag, which David proceeded to wave as he galloped around the ring. Tailor, who normally doesn't suffer fools gladly, seemed to sense the symbolism of the moment, and galloped on as if he did this every day.

Jim later said that as he stepped into the ring, an enormous security guard said, "Hang on, mate, you can't go in there." Jim replied, "you're not big enough to stop me," and performed a baton pass with the flag that would have made our 4 X 100 meter relay jealous.

There was a moment just before the three medal winners, David, Andrew, and Mark stepped on the podium today when I thought to myself, "what a brain trust." Three of the best horseman the world has ever seen, separated by the color of their medals, but united by their respect for each other, and their love for horses.

I can't close without mentioning what an outstanding job the Australians have done here. They are a warm, cheerful, friendly, engaging people, and they have been able to show it. The one thing that really struck me is what sports fans these Aussies are, and what good sports they are. They enjoy every moment of the performance, and are genuinely pleased for athletes from whatever country when they go well. The atmosphere here has been fabulous this week, and these must be the best Olympics ever held.

The atmosphere and team spirit behind the scenes of the U.S. team were equal to the occasion and are widely credited with our success. We are proud of our horses and riders for sure, but we should be equally proud of the grooms, vets, blacksmith, staff, and coach Mark Phillips.

As usual, Karen O'Connor had the last word. When congratulated on getting a team Bronze, the supporter added, "and an Individual Gold, too." "Hey," said Karen, "that Gold is a team medal, too!"

GREETINGS FROM JEREZ*

By the summer of 2002, I was coaching the Canadian Team, and was getting them ready for the World Championships in Jerez, Spain. When the U.S. Eventing Association magazine approached me about doing the same sort of articles I had done in Sydney, I was a little reluctant. Time constraints might prevent me from getting them in on time, or in as complete a fashion as I might like. But Jo Whitehouse and her wonderful staff at the USEA understood the problems, and on that basis I went ahead. "All this stuff is wandering around in my head while it is happening anyway," I thought. "I might as well have a place to store it."

*Reprinted by permission of United States Eventing Association.

I obviously get a kick out of these big international horse events. The opportunity to see so many good horses and riders in one place is fun, of course, but equally as interesting is the stuff that you know is going to happen. Putting on one of these championships or Olympic Games is like staging D-Day. The only thing you know for sure is that it won't go according to plan, and when the plan unravels, I will be there with a laptop and a sense of humor.

The Games in Sydney were admirably well organized. The World Championships in Jerez, on the other hand....

September 10, 2002

Greetings from Jerez. In my spare time, I will try to give you some of the stuff you won't get from the regular reports. Don't expect them every day, as if I get too tired, I'll just blow the project off. Feel free to send them on to anyone you think might enjoy them.

I am really looking forward to this event. It is something new, and that always gets me going. Every dog is brave in his own backyard, but it takes a special kind of horse and rider to step off the plane, take a look at the course and say, "Hey, really big, hard jumps that no one in the world has ever jumped before. Cool! I can hardly wait!" There aren't many around with that sort of attitude, but that is what it takes.

The Canadian contingent met me at the airport and led me out to the Hertz lot, where I get my first clue about how my week is going to go. Every form is filled out by hand, from the back of a minivan. Painstakingly. By hand. When the keys are finally handed to me, I am assured it will be in parking space B-4. Not a chance. First of all, there *is* no B-4. And, of course, the car closest to the spot has no resemblance to the grey four-door jelly bean I was promised. I resort to walking down the parking rows, punching the automatic door opener until I hear a clicking noise. There it is, in the Avis parking lot. So I pull out onto the Jerez road, feeling like I am dealing with my jet lag pretty well so far.

It is a strange feeling to be whizzing down a four-lane highway with road signs in a foreign language, listening to music I have stolen from the Internet and "burned" to my own CD, which is playing in a French car, rented in Spain, designed by Japanese, built in Portugal, and fueled by diesel imported from Iraq, which we are preparing to bomb the bleep out of at the earliest opportunity. I just hope they wait until I can get home before they push the button.

Jerez is a strange mixture of old Moorish architecture, and new cement blocks. Think El Cid meets Leonid Brezhnev and you've got it. There is a perceptible haze over the city, but not from the traffic, although there is enough of that to go around. (And around. Traffic in the city is mainly regulated by traffic roundabouts, which is like putting rabbits in charge of the lettuce patch, where Latin drivers are concerned.) No, the real reason there is a haze is because everyone smokes. Everyone. All the time. Everywhere.

The next thing you notice is that everyone has a cell phone. All the visitors have rented them for the duration, but don't know how to work them, so there is a continuous, curious series of electronic, warbling tones that spread through a group, followed by an extraordinary St. Vitus dance performed by those who think the call might be for them, but can't remember if they hung the phone on their belt, in a pocket, or wherever. Usually the call is for them. Everybody talks on their phone. A lot.

It is hot here during the day, but not unbearable, and the rumor is for temps in the low 80's by the weekend. The Spanish have not changed their attitude since the last time I was here. Charming, cosmopolitan, friendly, and totally detached from any suspicion of hustle. If you want accreditation? One hour minimum, to produce information that is already stored in their computer. Lost your bag? Count on days, not hours. (Although how you can misplace a large green Orvis bodybag escapes me). Anyway, I am not totally stupid. I packed two day's clothing in my backpack, just on the off chance someone might misplace my luggage.

The stores and restaurants open late in the morning, close for siesta, and reopen late. The dinner hour begins at nine p.m., and if you are so bold as to show up then, you will get the sort of smile reserved for the simpleminded, and be told to come back "in a few moments." That is 45 minutes, for those of you who do not speak Spanish, are hungry, or both. (Note to Jim: the Spanish don't do onion rings...those are either octopus, squid, or white, garlic-flavored bicycle tires, fried in batter. Where did you think you were, the Coach Stop in Middleburg?)

The stables are rudimentary, but sufficient. 12 by 12, with solid sides, and a tent roof. The electrical system works so far, but a lot of the grooms have just unpacked their stall fans, so watch for fireworks soon, once all those transformers get plugged in.

The biggest problem is the bathrooms. There aren't any. I mean none. As you can imagine, this has caused a fair amount of comment in the Chef de Equipe's meetings.

Only the Eventing, Dressage, and Vaulting horses are in the compound, and it is crowded already. The main exercise area is about the size of a large polo field, so there is not much elbow room. Tempers have not started to fray yet, but it is only Tuesday, so stick around.

Anyway, Dressage is already cranky, since for the first time in recorded memory some horses were actually inspected and may have actually been found to be, gasp, lame. Severe remonstrations are of course being made, so don't expect anyone to be eliminated just yet.

The footing is wonderful turf for the outside areas, and pretty good sand rings for the dressage areas. The Eventers will be on turf for both the dressage and show jumping phases, in the smaller stadium (seats about 2,500), and the main arena is sand.

The opening ceremonies were obviously designed by the local Chamber of Commerce. It was 55 minutes by my watch before the first horse "act" started. This topped off several soporific speeches in three languages (Spanish, Basque, and Other). As icing on the cake, the King of Spain pronounced the World

Equestrian Games open in the same tone of voice that Al Gore used to congratulate Dubya on his election. Where is P. T. Barnum when you need him?

One can but hope that with their usual unerring instinct the FEI once again bollixed up their TV contract, so that the sporting world was spared this latest edition of FEI-induced 18th Century razzle-dazzle.

A fairly knowledgeable crowd seems to be on hand, since the biggest applause of the evening went to the artillery team that broke its singletree after the first turn of the drill ride, but persevered. The army sergeant reminded me of Ben-Hur, as he went shooting out the front of the gun carriage. He plowed a bit of a furrow in the sand, but no harm done.

Things should pick up a bit tomorrow, when the Eventers walk the X-C course and have their vet exam. The rumor before the teams got here was that the Event would be a dressage competition, but the few who have snuck out for a peek at the course have come back looking a little green around the gills, so rumor is once again probably wrong.

It is a toss-up for the title of "most harassed-looking," between Mark Todd in his new role as coach of the Kiwis, trying to deal with Blythe Tait and Andrew Nicholson, and Wayne Roycroft. Wayne is caught between getting his defending Olympic Gold medalists ready to run, and dealing with a mindset at the FEI Bureau that has basically thrown the future of eventing to the International Olympics Committee (IOC) wolves.

Latest joke heard in the competitor's bar has Wayne Roycroft complaining to William Shatner that there are whites, blacks, orientals, and others shown on Star Trek, but no Eventers. "But Wayne," says Shatner, "Star Trek is set in the future!"

The buzz in the administrative offices is that the Basque separatists are planning something explosive for Saturday, so the horses will go out to the X-C area in several armed convoys. Welcome to the wonderful world of sport in the 21st Century...more as it occurs to me.

Greetings from Jerez. This little missive may be shorter, as I think I overdid the all-purpose brown last night. This morning we had an interminable meeting where not much was decided, and then piled into buses for the 45-minute ride to the cross-country site.

Anyone who thought this was going to be a dressage competition has had their consciousness elevated. On the ride home on the bus, several of the Western European riders looked as if they had just seen Elvis!

This is a true four-star course. It is big, square, built over much more undulating terrain than we had been led to believe, and asks the right questions, without the endless repetition of narrow jumps that has been the recent norm. Mike Tucker, the course designer, has a keen eye for rising and falling ground, and he has made good use of it. In addition, he knows what horses feel like when they get tired, and there are plenty of places, especially in the second half of the course, where riders on tired horses had better go the long way around the situation.

Roads and tracks are on packed gravel, which is going to be quite stinging for the horses, and is causing some concern. The steeplechase and X-C tracks are turf, on a prepared surface, so it will be a bit firm but level and with a bit of give in it.

The weather was in the high 80s by the time we got there, so with their usual attention to detail, the organizing committee made sure that there was neither food nor water for at least a 25-mile radius. I suppose it makes sense, when you remember that there are no porta-potties there either.

We made it back in time for the vet check, where all the horses looked really well. My official reason for being here is to coach the Canadian team. The protocol at the vet check is for the coach to walk up to the side of the jogging lane as his first team horse is presented. You stand there alone while the Ground Jury inspects your team, so it is a quick interval of peace and seclusion during an otherwise busy time. It was a poignant moment for me, to think I was standing where my father had stood, at the Helsinki Olympics, 50 years ago this summer. I know Dad and Mom are watching. I hope they enjoy the show.

SEPTEMBER 12, 2002

Greetings from Jerez. The first day of Eventing dressage is over, and went well. The judging is a bit biased towards "halos," but no more than normal and in many cases has actually been fairly perceptive. I know you can get all that stuff from the Internet, so I will skip that and cut to the chase.

Most of the riders' morale has started to improve, as they have now seen the X-C course for the second time and it now appears difficult, but no longer impossible. There are so many imponderables (heat, footing, shadows on the jumps, etc.) that most of the riders are basically saying, "The hell with it, I'm just going to go!" which is the right frame of mind, anyway.

The terrain reminds me a bit of the hill country north of San Antonio, with mesquite, pirul, eucalyptus, and cork trees in abundance, set in large brown fields. The native grasses are dry and sere at this time of year, so there is a strange juxtaposition of bright green turf on the galloping lanes, and dead, brown gramma grass. There is a metaphor in there for the interaction of mankind with his environment, but I am too jet-lagged to figure it out.

Speaking of jet lag, it is a real problem over here, as we all work 18-hour days, and wind up skipping every other meal. By now no one is hitting on all their cylinders. There is a Macdonald's just around the corner, but I haven't figured out how to say "super size it" in Spanish yet. As if missed meals weren't bad enough, throw in the normal propensity of the horse world to imbibe, and the possibilities for confusion and misunderstanding are endless. The organizing committee has basically thrown up their hands, knocked the top off a bottle of sherry, and given up making any sense of this circus.

For example, the saga of the porta-potties continues. The stable compound was rocked about midmorning by an explosion of some consequence. The first diagnosis was a terrorist bomb set off by the Basque Separatists, but further investigation revealed that it was a methane explosion, set off by someone sneaking a cigarette in the only operational porta-potty on the grounds. That will teach him to (1) quit smoking and (2) avoid the lentil soup in the competitor's tent. There is a rumor going around that the Croatian team (yes, I'm serious, would I kid about the Croatians riding at speed over four-foot high fences set in concrete?) has filled a spare stall with Kitty Litter, but I am afraid to ask.

The organizing committee has made everything as complicated as possible. At the World Championships, there will be a lot of competitors, right? They will all need food at some point. Are you with me so far? So, the competitor's food tent is as far as humanly possible from the stables. We're talking a half a mile here, folks. But get this...when you get there, there is no door that will allow you into the food tent. Oh, nooooo, too simple.

You have to climb over two security fences, basically break out of the secure competitors' compound, and come around to the door on the public side of the fence. Once there, you will be, of course, hassled at the door if you do not have the correct credentials and meal tickets. It is indeed surreal to see the Spanish security guards helping a little old lady break through the fence, and then smile as you climb over the fence, back into the secure area, after a lunch of mystery meat and unwashed fruit. If the turista ever strikes the World Equestrian Games, the Basques are going to be put to shame.

Now, let me see, what else? Oh, yes, note to Jim: that blue circle thingy? The one with the red line across it? That does not mean "reserved for jet-lagged Canadian coach." It means "no parking...period."

So now you understand how it was today that I met "La Gura" ("the hook"). But at the same time, how else would I have been exposed to the one element of this country that works with a frightening, Teutonic efficiency? There were some nice motor-cycle storm troopers near my late, lamented parking place, who knew all about the grey Hertz four-door jelly bean that had been subjected to La Gura. "Go to this address, bring lawyers, guns, and money,' they said with an evil glint in their eyes. "But, but," I expostulated in my schoolboy Spanish, "what about la siesta?"

"Oh, no problemo, Senor, eeees always abierta" they chuckled. So, off I went in a taxi, clutching my passport and a handful of Euros. When I arrived at the appointed location, I was swept into a cement cubicle, where a Gilda Radner look-alike with coke bottle lenses checked my passport, looked me up in the computer, took my 57 euros, stamped my papers, printed my receipt, handed me my keys, and pointed out my car, all in the space of a minute and a half. If the WEG organizing committee had Gilda running this circus, you can bet there would be enough porta-potties, by God! And, she would be standing in there to make sure you washed your hands, too!

Anyway, no harm, no foul. It is late here, and I have to sleep fast, to catch up. More later.

SEPTEMBER 13, 2002

Greetings from Jerez. With all the complaining I have been doing, we should not lose sight of the fact that there are some wonderful sights here for a horse lover. The first impression I got was how much the quality of the horses improves, each time I come to one of these things.

The eventers are truly athletic movers, most of them look fit, and they are very sound. This is a tribute to two things: (1) training methods have improved over the last few years—more and more coaches can produce these creatures in top condition—and (2) the increasing use of intra-articular injections to control arthritic conditions. A side effect of number 2 is that the average age of the horses has been going up for the last 10 years. Sixteen- and 17-year-olds are no longer the exception, if not yet the rule.

The Grand Prix dressage horses here this week are built on a lighter, more athletic frame, and the riding has improved across the board. There is a refreshing lack of the horrible kicking-and-pulling that used to be the norm, and these horses don't just walk, trot, and canter, they *dance!* The fad of pulling their head down between their knees seems to be dying out (thank God!), and the riders have their horses more "up" in front, with the poll truly the highest point of the horse's body. Thus they can show an increased lightness, some extravagant forward motion, and especially some passage and piaffe that will take your breath away.

But for my money the cutest horses here are the vaulters. They are mostly enormous Belgians, Percherons, or mixed draft horses, and probably average 1,500 pounds. Their sole job is to canter counterclockwise in a 20-meter circle for hours on end, while these waifs in spandex we call "vaulters" practice their gyrations. They have enormous, placid eyes, loppy great ears, and the world's sweetest attitude towards the children who swarm over, under, and around them. Their backs are quite flat, which I suppose is a comfort when one is about to do a triple Salkow, or whatever it is that they do during their routines.

The endurance and drivers are not in evidence, and the show jumpers have not arrived yet, as they all go during the second week.

Oh, yes, here is a verbatim transcript from the event athletes' press conference last night, after the first day's dressage scores were posted, with Phillip Dutton in the lead with a 33 and change:

Q: Phillip, you are listed as an individual, not as a member of the Australian team. Why is that?

A: Dutton: (*deadpan*) You'll have to ask the selectors.

Q: When did you find out that you had come all this way to be an individual at the WEG, after winning two Olympic Gold team medals in 1996 and 2000?

A: (*deadpan*) Last night.

Q: Did they give you any reason why you were left off the team?

A: (*deadpan*) They said my dressage wasn't good enough.

The background to this is that this time the Australian Gold Medal machine might have let its hubris outstrip its horsemanship. They announced last winter that anyone who did not score lower than 50 in the dressage tests this spring would not be considered for the team. They forgot that horses are not machines, and are paying the price now for looking at the scoreboard rather than the horses. It is not the first time selectors have picked the wrong rider, and anyway there is a long hot way to go to the medal ceremony on Sunday. But the rest of us are having a good laugh at the Aussies right now.

I haven't really gotten attuned to the rhythm of life here, since I keep such strange hours. But the one thing I do like is that the Spanish are very family oriented. They might go out to dinner at 11 p.m., but the full kit and caboodle comes along...stumpy, ancient grannies in black lace, duennas for the children, nannies for the infants, sullen-faced teenagers (that part is universal, for sure), aunts and uncles, the whole catastrophe.

The streets of Jerez are full of horse-drawn carriages, much like Central Park. The horses all have bells on their harness, which lends a slightly unusual background noise to the usual grumble of city traffic, rather like hearing Christmas carols on the Fourth of July. Now, where you have horses, you have horse...Well, you catch my drift.

I know, I know, I promised no more bathroom humor. But you do have to wonder about a culture that has one porta-potty for the entire stable area, but employs an army of sanitary workers to go around after the horses and make sure no horse apple is left unpicked. I mean that sucker barely hits the ground before the Spanish Siamese twins, Hose-A and Hose-B, are there with brooms and shovels. I thought about hiring them to follow me around, but I can't figure out how to say that in Spanish without either getting beat up, or propositioned. Anyway, I had to leave most of my Euros with Gilda yesterday, to get my car out of jail, so I would not be able to afford it.

Greetings from Jerez. Not much to say tonight, not because nothing went on today, but because I am pretty much brain-dead. I mentioned earlier the insane hours people work here, and it is catching up with me.

The course was every bit as difficult as we had thought it would be. The distressing thing is that most of the riders went out on course as if they were going to jump all the fast ways and make the time. And this over a very difficult course in unusually warm conditions. There have been some articles recently to the effect that we are currently producing good riders, but not good horsemen. That argument got a shot in the arm today. Even though the FEI has dumbed down the physical demands of the speed and endurance test, it is still the complete test of horse and rider, and has to be taken seriously.

When I walk a four-star course with people, I make the point that the extra 30 seconds on the steeplechase phase is the longest 30 seconds of their lives. That is why the speed around a championship course is harder to make than the speed around a three-star course, and the jumps seem harder. Same required speed, same height, same spread, but harder to do, because of the extra length of the steeplechase. It should not take an equestrian genius to figure that out. Add this into an equation that already features unusually warm temperatures and you have the makings of a really difficult event. When that sort of scenario presents itself, caution, not careless abandon is the order of the day. Unfortunately, caution was in short supply. Far too many riders overestimated their, and their horse's, capabilities today.

There were too many riders who did not take into account the extra difficulty of a championship, and they and their horses got caught out. There is only so much the officials, technical delegates, and designers can do to protect the image of the sport. The rest is up to the riders, and the many of these riders were a little short of horsemanship today.

This is not to take away from the riders who went well. As usual, when they got it right, they looked as if they were doing another sport than the rest of the world. Kim Severson Vinoski (she tells me she will go back to her maiden name after this season), Phillip Dutton, John Williams, William Fox-Pitt, and Jean Teulere come to mind. Sort of like the nursery school rhyme...when she was good, she was very good, and when she was bad, she was horrible.

The good news is that the horses seem pretty comfortable in the barn tonight, and are not as jarred as I had expected.

There must be something in the air...even the Internet is experiencing bad Fung Shui tonight, so it will probably be Sunday night before you get this...sorry about that. I need my beauty rest, and I am going to get some. More later.

SEPTEMBER 15, 2002

Greetings from Jerez. There is no tension like the tension in the rider's faces on Sunday morning, before the final Veterinary Inspection. They all hate it, because it is the only part of the competition where they do not control the outcome. They all know the purpose is correct, they do not want to do away with it, they do not want to change it or lower the standard of care somehow, they just hate it.

The Ground Jury set a good standard, I thought. They did not expect your horse to be clinically sound, but if your horse had a hitch in his getalong, leave him in the stall.

There was a small but highly knowledgeable crowd gathered to watch. If someone there in that crowd sneezed, the whole Eventing world would catch cold. The sport is becoming increasingly professional. This does not just mean prize money, but rather all the support that goes with a professional sports franchise. Most of the successful teams bring their own farriers, vets, equine physiotherapists, and some even bring human physical experts...credit Dr. Craig Ferrell, the USOC doctor for the U.S. team, for helping Amy Tryon to get through the final day, after a crashing fall on Saturday.

But with all that, the Eventing world is still a group of good sports. When a horse trots away from the jury and shows the results of its exertions, a susurrus of concern goes through the competitors and support staff gathered to watch. Imprecations are muttered, rosaries are touched, and invidious comparisons are made that so-and-so "was worse than that and they let *him* through." Then a roar as the announcer says "accepted." I watched an Australian, an Englishman, and an American while a horse from a fourth nation was presented and was a little rough around the edges. From the body language, you would not have been able to tell which was which, and they all jumped and pumped their fists when the horse was accepted.

What made me notice this was yesterday during the cross-country, while I was watching the television in the tent in the vet box. If you are a real fan, and you are granted one wish, get a ticket that will allow you to sit in the competitor's tent during a four-star team championship, with a clear view of the TV screen. The comments are rare, pungent, funny, and usually right on the button. But there is no edge to the chatter...most of the people in the tent have, at one time or another, been out there, so they know what they are watching.

No matter who is on course, the entire group in the tent is on their side. Let a horse start to get behind the rider's leg, and you have never seen such body language and elbow waving, or heard such a cacophony of cluckings, growlings, and "gaaawoooonnnn's" in your life. These people just like to see good horses ridden well. They don't look at the flag on the saddle cloths.

Four-star championships are a little like a heavyweight boxing match. We are in the closing rounds now, every one is tired, the momentum has changed back and forth a couple of times, and the final bell just rang. The title will go to the rider, and the team, that reaches down into themselves a little deeper, and finds the strength and the confidence to do their best for one more day. The administrative staff has done all the planning, coaches and trainers have done all they can do, and family and friends are off in the corners, nervously pacing, because they can't do anything.

Now it is up to the riders, and, of course, the horses. That's the way it should be.

SEPTEMBER 16, 2002

Greetings from Jerez, and points west. Some of this is written on my way back to the land of Coca-Cola, suspended 37,000 feet above the Atlantic Ocean in an aluminum tube that was built by low-cost suppliers. Plus, there is a very ethnic looking fellow two rows back, with a diaper on his head, and some very funky track shoes. Hard to catch up on your power naps, with that on your mind.

Also, some of this is late, due to computer difficulties beyond my control. The Luddites had a point. They definitely had a point.

I am still laughing to myself about the early veterinarian's meeting this morning. Remember how I told you that jet lag makes people act weird? Remember how many horses are on the grounds, that are through with their competition? All you need to do to ship your horse home is to get the vet papers and you are good to go. See where I am going with this?

Now, one would think the Organizing Committee would have prepared for the torrent of paperwork. Well, one would think wrong. All the vets and managers coming to the head health paper honcho's office were probably prepared for a bit of a wait, but "maybe tomorrow" was most definitely not acceptable.

Stress makes people do strange things. I mean, what would you have bet that it would be the Swiss vet who would snap? Yup, totally lost his neutrality. At the same time, it was instructive how effective a negotiating tactic it is to pound the living daylights out of a wall right behind the head health paper honcho's head with a chair, while screaming, "Gottfordammurung, mit schnitzel," or some such. I suppose it was the sincerity with which this sentiment was delivered that had such a transformational effect on the process. The Swiss got their papers in a heartbeat.

Jim Wolf, the director of Eventing for the USET, takes a more subtle approach to this sort of thing. He hired a very large, very thuggish-looking man to come into the office with him, and stand with his arms crossed and a scowl on his face, right behind Jim. Then Jim leans over and hisses that this guy is Jim's assistant, and he is going to sit on the health paper honcho's face until he stops breathing, or he produces the health papers, whichever comes first. Efficiency is such a marvelous thing, don't you think?

You know all about the winners and losers by now, especially the U.S. team's Gold Medal, so let's talk about some of the other stuff. Jim Wolf is even more superstitious than I am. He had 50 bottles of champagne put on ice Saturday evening, then locked it up, and wouldn't let anyone see it until after the medal ceremony. Huh? Oh yeah, and had to buy another 20, before the night was over. That tent was rocking.

Favorite views of the evening? Either Karen O'Connor getting William Fox-Pitt's autograph on her, uuuhhh, lower back. Way lower back. Or, Mark Phillips, obviously in a good mood, signing autographs on young ladies' bosoms. You shoulda been there.

Everyone is pleased by the results, even if their teams or riders did not do as well as they might have hoped. The teams involved in the medals are the real thing. The three individuals are good riders who have all paid some serious dues and finally caught lightning in a bottle. All in all, the winners validated the competition.

The atmosphere in the stands during the show jumping was the same as in the cross-country tent, which is to say, enthusiastic and supportive. It was a tough, fair show jumping course, with some good questions, and two interesting option lines involving short and long routes. If you took the easier and lower, but longer, lines you were going to get some time faults. Those lines were why there were so many time faults, and partly why double clears were in such short supply.

The designers have figured out that four-star horses are tired on Sunday afternoons, and thus they do not come off the ground with the same snap as on Saturday morning. Plus, they do not jump as clean as they did at their last horse trials. In addition to all this eventers do not ride show jumping well if they feel hurried. So, if the designer can make them hurry a little, well, it can look like Bowling for Dollars out there.

The outcome of this subplot was that there were a lot of jump and time faults, which materially affected the outcome, but it was fair, and it was the same for everybody. The people in the competitor's stands knew this, and were really doing their best to cluck, groan, and elbow-flap everyone into a clean round. When it worked, they erupted, and when it didn't work, they turned away as the rider walked out the walkway, not in disgust but in sympathy, and left the riders who had disastrous rounds alone with their grief.

A NFL coach, the late George Allen, said, "Every time you lose, you die a little." The looks on those unfortunates' faces told you they were dying inside, and there was nothing anyone could say or do to make it better. While we are quoting famous coaches, one of my favorites is by Bert de Nemethy, who said, "A good feeling after the round is better than any ribbon."

What he did not say, but could have, is that there is no feeling worse than letting your horse and yourself down by not riding up to your potential. The hard part is not that you had a bad round. The hard part is that you did not ride as well as you are capable of riding. Take it from me, that is the part that goes through your mind 50 years later, and makes you sick at your stomach all over again.

The first big competition I ever won, I didn't win; some one else actually lost it. I caught a glimpse of his face as I stepped up to get the trophy, and realized that when you win something big, and you are standing on a victory podium, you are standing on the ruins of someone else's dreams. It was never the same for me again.

But what was the same was the spirit at the party. It was a relief to me to know that loud talk, red faces, and public drunkenness are still a part of the Eventing scene. I can call to mind several who scored a triple, on that basis. I did not quite get myself to that condition, because I had such an early flight on Lufthansa, of which more in a moment. But I did have enough champagne that I decided that I had better skip the finals of the Grand Prix

Dressage. It did not start until nine that night and was not over until after eleven-thirty p.m. I told you about those brutal hours? That's what I mean. But I heard there wasn't an empty seat in the house, and the town was still rocking when I drove through the streets early the next morning.

You gotta love Spain. This is a different culture for sure. Where else do you know of that has a 24-hour flamenco TV channel? Sort of Latin MTV. Have you ever seen a flamenco performance? What happens is that some old guys sing, prance, and gyrate around, while several ladies watch in stunned adoration and amazement, and indulge in some serious syncopated hand-clapping. One thing you have to say, nobody claps on the back beat in Spain. I mean, these people know how to clap.

I do like the fact that in Spain, youth is only a prelude to maturity, not a desirable condition. There aren't many young fla-menco singers or dancers. These guys are in their 50s and 60s and they haven't seen their toes for a good 20 years. If you are slender in Spain, it just means you are not prosperous, not that you are fashionable. And the ladies, well, they are busmatic, and they have the white lace and low necklines to prove it. The guitar music sounds like something out of a spaghetti western, and the singing has a strange resemblance to the singing at a Navajo rain dance I went to as a child. It is a little hard for someone from Upperville, VA, by way of Milford, Kansas, to appreciate.

But these guys go at it. The songs go on for quite some time (unrequited love, like everything else in this country, takes a while.) The rhythms are sinuous, and they mostly sing without a microphone, so they really have to project their voices. When they are done, water is pouring off them, and the ladies' mascara has long since given up and headed south. Hard to see how they keep their shapes, with all that exercise, but they manage.

I suppose I should not be too hard on flamenco. We would get the same reaction from the Spanish if we put B. B. King and Muddy Waters up there. It is a cultural thing, and not all these things translate very well. Sometimes, after a couple of all-pur-pose dark browns, my mean streak starts to surface, and I ask one of my unsuspecting English friends to explain cricket to me.

Can't be done. See what I mean about culture? But that's OK, because we can't explain American football to them either. You gotta go with what you know.

I can't say flamenco was my favorite. What were my favorite parts? It would be a toss-up between that Spanish army guy, getting Ben-Hur'ed out of his chariot during the opening ceremonies, when his singletree broke, and Karen O'Connor, getting her, ahem, lower back autographed at the competitor's party.

But my real favorite was being able to spend so much time surrounded by wonderful horses. Just wonderful, big-moving, sound, fabulous horses, everywhere you looked. That was the best part.

Anyway, after the usual "alarum and excursions" I arrived safely (somewhat to my bleary eyed surprise) at Dulles, only to find, you guessed it, no bag. Yup, lost it again. The head Lufthansa Baggage Nazi behind the counter took my details, and noticed that they had lost my bag on the way out as well. He was nice enough to apologize profusely for the inconvenience.

"Not to worry," I said, "I'm getting used to it."

So I'm home safely. I hope you had as much fun reading these little missives as I did writing them. See you soon.

GREETINGS
FROM ATHENS

After the Olympics in Sydney, I was hired by the Canadian team to prepare them for the 2004 Olympics in Athens. By the time I got to Athens, I was sufficiently advanced in my computer skills to be posting the daily articles on my own website. I was also out of control. I must have been reading too much S. Hunter Thompson at the time. The nice thing about writing for your own weblog is that you are basically writing a diary. The bad thing, of course, is that you tend to forget that someone else may read it. Fortunately, my more scandalous and non-PC parts were cut in the editing process.

Later on in this chapter I will make a reference to "Horsegate." Like most of these things it started out simple, and went complex in a hurry. The short version is that Bettina Hoy, from Germany, came into the final round in first place, but circled through the start line twice. This is a no-no, but the Ground Jury missed it, then the other teams protested, and then, and then...

And then, of course, we had a 90-day saga to decide the winner. Once you get bureaucrats and lawyers together, nothing happens quickly. However, that was all in the future. While I was writing this from Athens, I was surrounded by fabulous horses, people I have known all my life, all the confusion that accompanies the Olympics, and the thrill of being at an historic occasion.

As you will notice, I was having a ball at the Olympics...except for the frozen octopus.

AUGUST 9, 2004

Greetings from Athens. As my time permits, I am going to keep a blog about my travels. I want to point out right away that any connection between my blog and reality is accidental. Still, if it didn't happen this way, it should have.

I won't bother with the results, since most of the world will be watching on simulcasts anyway. This will be more in the way of a personal diary. Remember that guy who worked for Clinton, testified under oath, and then had his diary subpoenaed? Asked to explain the discrepancy between his sworn testimony and his diary, he admitted to lying to his diary. That's my kind of diary. (Clinton had that effect on people, didn't he? "It depends on your definition of the word 'diary'") Anyway, I just started this diary, and I've lost my train of thought already. Where was I? Oh, yeah, leaving for Athens.

My paranoia factor stays pretty high under normal circumstances, so you can imagine how badly I was rubbernecking by the time I got to Dulles today. I was on my way to Athens, which figures to be Mecca Central for Achmed and His Band of Merry Men, and I was a little spooked!

It didn't do my morale much good to board the plane with two guys with beards, turbans, several MacDonald bags, and B.O. that made my eyes water. They moved in behind me and got into a hissing contest. It is hard to eavesdrop on an argument in a language like Farsi or Pashto, as you don't know what the cognates mean. Did he really say, "Death falls from the skies on devil dogs," or "Death smells better than the skin on these hot dogs?" It's a good thing the air marshals took them away. By the time they slapped the cuffs on the two perps, most of the guys in my cabin were taped up, had their blocking assignments and were slapping high fives and saying stuff like "let's roll."

The whole scene was a bit too much for me, but after the attendant hit me with the defibrillator paddles the second time, things started looking up. When she asked me if there was anything she could do, I pointed weakly at the drinks tray, and was rewarded with enough all-purpose brown to ensure a significant nap. Let me get back to you about that...whatever that was...lemme see, I wonder what happens if you pull this lever here? Ahhh, that's better.

August 10, 2004

Greetings from Athens. "Welcome home," the sign says as you walk down the concourse at the Athens airport. Makes you feel right at home, if you are into olive drab and submachine guns. Every one here is in some kind of uniform. The soldiers and security forces are in their berets, carrying hand guns with one in the chamber, and the "Olympic Family" is in khakis and polo shirts. Every four years, Olympic Organizing Committees pay megabucks for people to design things that make everyone look equally like a dork. These shirts are several shades of blue on one arm, a white body in the middle (shows the pizza and coke stains better, doncha know), then going several shades of brown on the other arm.

Can't you just hear some prissy designer saying, "The dark blue is the Aegean, the brownish blue is the sewage effluent you see seeping from all those cruise ships in the harbor as you fly into the airport, the white is your face when you get my bill, and the browns are the noxious fumes from all the traffic on all the new freeways." Works for me.

Every country buys into this sort of thing. After one good look, you can pick out the Germans from a mile away (sort of a Zyklon-B mustard yellow), the Hungarians are in red gingham shirts and tasteful straw cowboy hats, and the Rooskies are in what can only be described as red-and-white Hawaiian. The desired result being that they look like Hawaiian dorks, I guess. I can hardly wait to see what I'm going to be wearing for the next 10 days.

After the uniforms, the next thing you notice is how young and fit every one looks. The kids are ready, and they look it. There is such an incredible array of body types here...4'9" Filipino weight-lifters, bikers, and runners, drawn like a wire, and one gorgeous blonde from the Russian women's basketball team. How did I know that? Well, I guessed. I mean, how many 6'10" girls do you see wearing a red-and-white Hawaiian shirt?

Another thing that hits you right away is the variety of languages that are being spoken. Polyglot doesn't begin to describe it. There is an impressive array of translators on duty all the time. Serbian, Croatian, Farsi, even Australian, they are all right here. I asked one of the Olympic Family ladies about getting my credentials, and she answered me in English, talked on her cell phone in Spanish, and flirted with one of the boys behind the counter in Greek...all at once. Pretty impressive. (Too bad she was giving me the wrong information.)

Did I mention the part where the Olympics are always screwed up behind the scenes? Count on it. "Oh, yes, you take this bus here for your credentials." Now you have to understand that your credentials are the Holy Grail, your Daddy's credit card, and the keys to the T-bird, all wrapped into one. No credentials? Then the Olympics are not happening for you, my friend.

The way it works, you get off the plane with your "combi-card" (combination Olympic data form and Greek immigration visa). No combi-card? No problem, just take this bus to the Olympic Village. Ooops, you can't use the Olympic bus if you don't have credentials. But I can't get to the Village to get my credentials if I don't use the bus, because no taxis are allowed, because of security concerns. But you need your credentials to use the bus. But I don't have my credentials...Well, after 45 minutes of this, I got on the bus. I didn't know it was the wrong bus yet. That came later.

But I had already had my first intimation that despite everything you have read about how these games are not ready, they are going to happen, and happen pretty well. It is going to work because the Greeks want it to work, and they are unfailingly charming, and helpful. When a snafu (that's Army talk for Situation Normal, All F****d Up) such as this develops, they simply help you game the system. "Oh, don't worry, Mr. Warfurd, I weell distract ze bus driver and you jus' get on, and no one weell notice." That sort of thing.

So I got on the bus, drove 45 minutes and got off the bus and into a block-long line to wait for my credentials. After a two-hour wait, I finally got to a young lady at a computer terminal, who said, "Oh, dear, you are in the wrong credential center for that sort of pass."

Now what? I asked. "You must go to the Olympic Village on the bus."

I mildly explained my bus problem, and a mischievous gleam came into her eyes. This was yet another illustration of why I think these Games are going to turn out pretty well. The Greeks have designed this perfect security cocoon, this vast, intricate, bureaucratic machine with all the attendant rules and regulations, and then they delight in showing you how to get around it.

"Wait here," my new best friend said. She came back with the Chief of *all* security for the Games.

"Yah, just come with me, I'm going to a meeting now, they'll let you in if you are with me," he said, and drove me to the Village.

He told me about some of the stresses and strains that the system is under right now. Three thousand athletes came into the Village today, and more on the way. To make me feel better, he told me that the U.S. Olympic Committee VP in charge of getting all the U.S. athletes credentialed had quit two weeks ago, and the U.S. system has crashed.

"That's probably causing you some problems," I perceptively mentioned.

"You have no idea," he said.

"Thanks for the ride," I said, and went inside to get my credentials.

I emerged 30 minutes later, grabbed a cab, and headed for the Equestrian venue at Marcopoulo (pronounced Mar-KOHP-olo). The highways and main venues look ready, but you don't want to look down any of the side streets. I got the feeling they have been sweeping a lot of things under the rug, in order to get the main things ready to go.

I wonder if we could get that judge in New York to let Martha Stewart do some early work release over here. You can never find a good feather duster when you need one, can you? Anyway, I made it to the stables, checked on the horses (I'm coaching the Canadian team), and grabbed a meal at the athletes dining hall. Maybe I shouldn't have done that.

I am what I ate, and I'm afraid. More tomorrow.

AUGUST 11, 2004

Greetings from Athens. They don't have much need for a weather-babe on the local TV stations here at this time of year. About once a week they can just say, "High's about 90 degrees today, and going down to 70 tonight. Some scattered high clouds after lunch." Marcopoulo is only one mountain ridge away from the Aegean, so there is always a nice breeze, and if you can find some shade, it is pretty comfortable. The nice thing about traveling is that when you get there, you are in a different place. The climate around Athens is euphemistically described as "arid." That means it is hot and dry, for those of you who have been watching too much *Access Hollywood*.

What this means is that the architecture is almost exclusively stucco and red tile roof, with wide, covered verandas. Athens is built on a very human scale. Most of the buildings downtown are only a few stories high, and show a refreshing lack of chrome and glass. The feel is similar to the area inland from San Diego, sere and dry, with little in the way of shade trees. There are plenty of fig trees and grape arbors on the outskirts of Athens. You know you are in a third-world country when the directions say, "Go along this road until you come to the fig orchard with sheep and goats in it, and turn left."

The downtown streets are clean, and you don't see any homeless vagrants around. Basically, about six months ago, this giant voice came out of the sky and said, "Yo, Nickolaides, get a job, or get out of Dodge!" The government was Socialist at the time they won the Olympic bid process, but even Socialists get heartless when NBC is about to show up on their doorstep. The recently installed Conservative government has naturally continued this policy. The only change being that they have increased the beatings during interrogation sessions.

At about the same time, the prostitutes union here threatened to go on strike (I don't care if you don't believe me...look it up...everyone else is unionized, why not the ho's?), but I noticed that concept fell off the TV screen quickly, so someone cut a deal somewhere. I would have loved to sit in on those negotiations between the politicians and the prostitutes...but I repeat myself.

What was the final clue to me that I was in a different country? I would have to say it was the sight of a whole octopus, shrink-wrapped and frozen, waiting in the freezer section of our local convenience store. No, now that you mention it, I haven't seen any roadkill. These people will eat anything. Can't anybody around here say "Angus"?

I was born and raised in Milford, Kansas, so when I go someplace like this my head is on a swivel. You are a loooooong way from Kansas, Jim-beau. I don't want to say that Milford was the most backward place in the world, but when I was growing up there, if you walked down the street with a 40-pound sack of Calf Manna on your shoulder on Friday afternoon, you were gonna get a date.

But there is a rumor going around that if I hang around here long enough, an Olympic Event is going to break out, and I wouldn't want to miss that. We haven't talked about the equestrian facilities yet, and I want to do that before the competition starts, since I won't have as much time later on. The actual facilities are state of the art. Built of tan stucco and red tile roofs, the center aisle stables are designed in blocks of four stable buildings, around a large courtyard. There are five of these stable compounds, which is not much, when you figure that the new race track next door has 1,800 stalls. The stalls are 12' by 14', with whitewashed stucco walls, high ceilings, and a fan in the wall at the back of each stall. There are 18 stalls in each building, plus equipment rooms, tack rooms, wash stalls, and an air-conditioned office.

The exercise rings are a space age mixture of sand and shredded felt, so you feel like you are walking on springs when you walk across them. There are separate competition arenas for the Dressage and the Show Jumping. The main Dressage arena is on the same kind of sand as the training arenas and the main Show Jumping arena is turf, so the footing in the competition arenas should not be a problem.

That's the good news. The bad news is that there are only two large working arenas, and four dressage training arenas for the entire cast of characters gathered here, so things are a bit claustrophobic. The estimate is for about 70 eventing competitors, if everyone that is entered shows up. Since the hacking is extremely limited, it will be a challenge to keep the horses and riders from going stir-crazy over the next few days.

And speaking of crazy, I have been going to these things for a while. My observation is that event riders react to stress the same way human beings do. Maybe more so. There is an interesting moment in every rider's life in a situation like this. Sometime over the next couple of days, every rider suddenly is going to look around and say, "Damn, I'm about to ride in the Olympics!" That's when the fun begins, because the stress level goes up exponentially from that point.

They all deal with it in different ways, mostly by drinking. The FEI controls the Olympic prohibited list for human medications and substances. They knew what they were doing when they left alcohol off that list, because most of the competitors would test positive! There is a café at the gate into the stable area, where they serve booze about 18 hours a day. When I left last night, the Brits and the Irish were having a good old-fashioned stress reduction session, and most of the small talk in the security lines this morning was of the "I feel positively beastly, what about you?" variety.

My team is a little sneakier than some. They had a pretty good pipe opener the night before I got here, based on the excellent logic that I might disapprove and so what I did not know couldn't hurt me. Plus, they would have time to get well before we started training seriously. It does not bode well when the Irish and Canadian grooms are already planning their devilment for the competitor's party. All I can say right now is it is gonna be expensive, it involves wheeled vehicles, somebody is going to break something, and the police are really going to be POed. I'll keep you posted about this one. In the meantime, I figure if I play my cards right, I can be somewhere else with a glass of brown when the cops come around looking for a "Responsible Party."

Speaking of which, booze has always played a big part where horse people are concerned. I didn't mention the U.S. team in the above list of miscreants solely because they just got here, and don't have their credentials yet. Anyway, they probably won't be able to top their stunt from the World Games two years ago. They missed their flight into Jerez, so had to take the train from Madrid. Stressed, hot, tired, dehydrated, no coach, no Chef d'Equipe, and with two weeks of per diem cash burning a hole in their pockets, well, what do *you* think happened? You got it...first class seats and champagne! Mucho champagne. Enough champagne that when you ask them about it, they all smile, and say, "Oh no, what you hear here, and what you say here, stays here, when you leave here!"

The U.S. team manager, Fiona Tibone, met the train that night, took one look at them spilling off the steps of the train, with a couple of them in a fireman's carry, and dialed the U.S. coach, Mark Phillips. "Hey, Mark, I think you had better reschedule the dressage training times tomorrow morning." Phillips of course inquired further, and when being told of the circumstances, merely asked, "Did they bring me any?" It may be the 21st Century, but horse people haven't changed much.

Another thing that hasn't changed is the effect of jet lag. I'm going to shut this down for the night, stretch out, listen to the crepitations of my old joints, and think about how much fun I am having, and the event hasn't even started yet

AUGUST 12, 2004

Greetings from Athens. One of the best things about the Olympics is that you see people you haven't seen for a long time. You walk around the corner and bump into someone you last saw four or eight years ago. The Olympics are a real gathering of the clan. As soon as the Olympics in Sydney were over, all the coaches and administrators from all of the horse world started planning and scheming to do as well, or better, in Athens. And they have all shown up here, to see how it comes out. Most of the riders are here now, and so one can start to get an idea of how teams look. The Brits look fabulous, as do the U.S. horses. I am coaching the Canadians, so of course I think they are looking good. I watched Andrew Hoy, captain of the Australian team and the Silver medalist from Sydney, warm up yesterday, and he must be one of my picks to place here. (No, I'm not ready to stick my neck out yet...get back to me after the vet check on Saturday afternoon.)

Pippa Funnel looks good, and her horse looks fit, but he would not be my choice to ride in a "short" format. Jean Tulure, the Gold medalist from the World Games two years ago, looks fit, but he might have had to run his horse one too many times in an FEI-induced, stupid scramble to qualify for Athens.

Kim Severson and Winsome Adante walked around this morning looking like front page news, and Carrick, John Williams' ride, has the same air of quiet confidence.

Blythe Tait and Andrew Nicholson are here for the Kiwis, and their horses seem well, but I have not seen them do any work yet. I'm sure those two will have their horses ready. I overheard a conversation between Jim Wolf, the U.S. Chef d'Equipe, and Mark Todd, who is now the coach of the New Zealand team. The conversation went something like this:

Jim Wolf: "Morning, Toddy."

Mark Todd *(all 6'2" of himself shriveled down to about 5'9," wearing his Maui Jim's at eight in the morning, looking like an albino prune, and very hung over)*: "Uummmph."

JW: "Toddy, now that you are coaching the Kiwis, I thought you'd be pacing yourself a little better."

MT: "Uh, yeh, when I was riding, I trained on beer and cigarettes, and it worked for me then. No reason to change now."

JW :"OK, have a good day."

MT: "Uummmph."

When they say consistency is the hallmark of champions, I'm not sure that is what they mean. I'm almost afraid to tell that story, as some of my young tigers are going to think, well it works for Toddy, why not for me? All I can say is, "The only time anyone else ever had a chance when Toddy was around was if he had drunk himself legless the night before...kids, don't try this in your living room."

I think the rider's focus is going to start to tighten now. They have been wandering around all week, full of restless, undirected energy. But the draw for the order of go is tomorrow at noon, the opening ceremonies are tomorrow night, and after that they will be too busy to be nervous. They are wound up now, and their horses are as fit as they are going to be this year. All they need is for someone to aim them, and to pull the trigger.

I mentioned earlier that I have been going to these things for quite a while. One of my earliest memories is of sneaking into the secure area around the Olympic torch at the 1948 Olympics in London. What was I doing there? Well, boys will be boys. One way or another, I have been to 11 Olympics. But no matter how many of these things you come to, there is always a thrill, a sense of history about to be made. I remember the British rider, Ginny

Holgate, telling me after her first Olympics in Los Angeles: "Jimmy, when I turned down the center line to start my dressage test, I have never felt such a sense of occasion!" A sense of occasion. What a wonderful expression, and so true. There is the feel of something historic in the air, and I am glad I am here to be a small part of it. I'm going to close for now with a quote from Cervantes' Don Quixote: "If thou are not versed in adventures, get thee aside and pray, whilst I engage these giants in combat."

These kids are going to literally trust their horses with their lives this week. You might say a prayer for them. I know I am going to.

I had meant to close out my blog for the night, but thought I might share this with you. After I posted to my website late this afternoon, I went down to the corner store (aka Octopus-R-Us). There was a palpable buzz in the air, and an unusual amount of people out and about at this time of day. I overheard someone with Olympic credentials and a heavy Australian accent ask the young lady behind the counter what was going on. The Olympic torch is passing through soon, she explained.

Will Rogers said, "We can't all be heroes, but we can all clap as they go by." And so it was that I stood on the curb and waved and clapped with the citizens of Marcopoulo as the torchbearer jogged steadily by. It came to me that our sport has gone through some wrenching changes over the past few years, and this was the reason. For a little while, our horses and riders will step out onto the world stage. For a little while, we will all be citizens of the world, and we can all clap and cheer as our heroes turn towards the entrance to the arena.

August 13, 2004

Greetings from Athens. We only worked the horses this morning, because the opening ceremonies are this evening, and it takes a while for all the thousands of athletes to assemble. I told them I would be just as happy here in the air-conditioning, serving as the emergency contact number for our team. Seeing as how they probably won't get home 'til after midnight, I thought that was a pretty good trade.

There is always something weird going on when the Olympics are involved; you just don't know what it is going to be yet. If you get this many people in one place, I will guarantee that something strange, or weird, or unlucky is about to happen. For example, Sara Cutteridge has had to withdraw from the British team. Her horse broke down doing dressage the first morning she got here. She is out, and Mary King will ride in her place. The British usually have some catastrophe like this happen to them. In 2000, Rodney Powell, a team member that year, took his horse for a walk the first morning he was there, slipped, fell, and Rodney broke his ankle. End of story.

One of my Canadian team members had his horse spook this morning while he was leading it to our daily team jog. He slipped on the pavement, and fell heavily on his side. He may or may not be OK for the official vet exam tomorrow. We'll just have to see how he feels. The moral of the story is don't count your chickens, especially when the Olympics are concerned.

Anybody who follows horses knows what a heartbreaking experience they can provide. August 13, 1919, is the day that the incomparable Man O'War lost to a horse named Upset. Man O'War must have been some horse. He was facing the wrong way when they started (they did not use starting gates in those days) and was giving up a ton of weight, and only lost by a neck. The following year he won a match race against a good horse by 100 lengths! His long-time groom, Will Harbut, said he was "the mostest hoss that ever was."

That might be so, but I saw Secretariat make his move going through the last turn in the Belmont, and leave the entire field behind. I saw Snowbound break down during the last round in 1968 in Mexico City, and jump the rest of the course on three legs and his heart, thus winning a Gold medal for Bill Steinkraus. Aherlich and Reiner Klimke did a test at the Los Angeles Olympics in 1984 that will always be my personal benchmark for dressage. Prince Panache and Karen O'Connor anchored the

U.S. event team in Sydney with the greatest display of moral and physical courage I have ever seen, on a day when anything less would have meant failure.

That may be why some of us keep coming back to these things. Every now and then a horse and rider will redefine excellence, and we treasure the memory and measure all that we see in the future by what we now know to be possible. That may be the answer to why we keep coming, the knowledge that something historic may happen, and we will be able to tell our fellow horse lovers that we were there the day that...

I have already mentioned how you run into people at the Olympics that you don't see very often. I ran into Daddy Stibbe this morning. He is Eddy Stibbe's father, and we are old friends. He is 82 now, mentally acute, but quite stooped, and he walks with a cane. Yet there he was early this morning, slowly making his way towards the exercise arenas. As horses came by he would pause and gaze at them with a soft, knowing, loving eye, still entranced by their power and beauty after a lifetime of watching them. I stood with him in a companionable silence for a moment, and then we just smiled at each other and went our appointed ways.

So I think I had better go my appointed way, and leave the rest of the story to unfold. The official course walk is tomorrow morning, and the vet exam in the afternoon. They are working on the Dressage arena now, watering, dragging and rolling it, and preparing the stands for the first day of competition. All the years of preparation, all the heartbreaks and triumphs, all the work and struggle are in the past now. All that remains is four days of competition in the heat of an Olympic summer here in Athens.

In his book *Supreme Command*, Eliot Cohen said "If you want to study the finest steel, best to search for the hottest furnace."

They are about to turn the heat up here, so sit back, click on the TV and while you are at it, you might set the air-conditioning a little cooler. We are about to study the finest steel that the horse world has to offer, in the ultimate crucible of sport...the Olympics.

Greetings from Athens. Let the Games begin! The riders got their ride times today, the Chef d'Equipes have determined their order of go within the teams, and everyone has at long last seen the cross-country course. I noticed that most of the riders' small talk has subsided now, as the true import of their task has started to sink in. Have you ever seen the dog that caught the car? "Now that I've got it, what am I going to do with it?" Like that.

Everyone that presented their horse to the Ground Jury at the vet exam got through today. That doesn't mean that there were no horses that weren't a little rough around the edges. But there were none that were "chicken-pickin'-corn-lame," and I thought the Ground Jury got it about right. Most of the teams look good and very fit.

Ian Stark, the long-time captain of the British team, is now coaching the Brazilians. I have to remember to ask him what he is feeding those horses. Their team uniform is white slacks with a neon lime-green blazer. The entire team is tall, skinny, good looking, and young. Ian has these horses wound up like a cheap watch, so at one point in the proceedings, three out of five of his horses were misbehaving. One was standing on his hind legs and boxing like a kangaroo, one was letting fly with both back feet, and one was towing his jockey across the warm-up area. For a moment, I had a mental picture of lime Popsicles being flung around the arena. Ian stepped in and squared things away, but not before the cognoscenti had a good laugh.

But that is all secondary to the main concern...the cross-country course. The track of the course basically starts out up a hill for about a mile and a quarter, turns 180 degrees, and comes back down the same hill following a similar track on the way back down. Right away this tells you several things: the jumps are going to look small on the way up, because the designer can't build a maximum fence; the track of the course is going to put a premium on fitness because the uphill part is so relentless; and finally, the same sort of jumps are going to be bigger and harder on the way back down, because the horses are starting to get tired. The jumps are beautifully designed and built, and should provide both a great spectacle for TV, and get the right result.

If I could only use two words to describe what the successful rider is going to display here those words would be "feel" and "concentration." Unlike past Olympics, there is nothing here that these horses and riders have not seen before. Years ago it was not unheard of to turn a corner, look at the next obstacle, and say to your self "What the heck is that thing? I've never seen anything like it before. How am I going to ride that?"

There is none of that here. There are several uphill bounces to a narrow jump, which is a standard question at the international level these days. However the jumps are a little bigger than usual, and the distances are just a trifle more forward and scopey. If you barf up any of these steps, you had better have another option in mind, because Plan A is no longer operational.

The first water jump is similar to the log-on-a-lump that we saw at the first water complex at Rolex this spring. It is much harder this time, because you now land on a grass slope, take three forward strides, jump a ramp with a 6'6" drop in to water, take three slightly forward strides across the water, and jump a boat-house corner with the red flag on the point. You land back in the water, and take two forward strides to an identical boathouse, with the white flag on the point. Both the houses are 3'9" and probably 5'6" where you jump them. Oh, did I mention that there is only about 4' of overlap between the two corners? You will really have to thread the needle.

Still, I think the majority of the competitors will go the straight route here. In fact, I think the majority of the field will be clear up to the turn at the top of the hill. Then the real Olympics start! There are several very big jumps on the way back down the hill, including one maximum drop. There is a coffin that would not have been out of place in any Olympic course over the last 50 years...it's that big! In addition, there are any number of places that a tired horse, or an inattentive rider, can have a refusal or a glance off.

To turn in a clear round here, the rider is going to have to "feel" his horse completely. I mean the horse's fitness, mental attitude, physical balance, the whole horse. Add to this that the design of the course is unusually demanding on the rider's concentration, and things start to get really hard. Given time, and a fit horse, there is no fence out there that all the horses and riders could not jump successfully. But you are in a hurry and, after five minutes of galloping or so, you are on a tired horse. So add all this up and you come up with an Olympic course which is not the biggest I have ever seen (that dubious honor goes to the 1960 Olympics in Rome) but will take a lot of jumping. However, I am convinced it will produce a good result.

But the end result of my day is that I am going to cut this short, post it, and grab some sleep. As the week progresses, you might check back through here, as I will add to and embellish this web log as time permits.

AUGUST 15, 2004

Greetings from Athens. The first day of dressage is over, and there were no surprises in the placings so far. This phase has begun to assume more and more importance over the past few years, and the riders with a flair for it have a definite advantage. The only joker in the pack is the weather, and I don't mean the heat. The wind came up about 10 a.m., and started howling a gale. The stadium is at the top of a hill, so it gets the full brunt of the wind. The flags were snapping, the flowers were swaying, and trash was blowing across the arena...all the things that event riders do *not* want to have happen. Several riders who could have legitimately expected to get good scores were adversely affected by the conditions.

Probably the most notable in this group was Blyth Tait, who has been going well all week. Reddy Teddy jigged into the arena, spooked at the stands, and proceeded to kick over the flowers and plastic letter at "A" as he started his entrance. After that, it would be safe to say that Blyth was engaged in damage control, rather than dressage. The look on his face as he left the arena would make your stomach knot. Here are the individual Gold medal winners from the Atlanta Olympics, and they are effectively out of the competition before they have jumped a fence.

I saw him later on and said, "Sorry, Blyth." "Yeah, well, what can you do?" said Blyth. We both just shook our heads and kept walking because we both know the sport. Blyth is one of the best riders in the world; he has spent four years of his life getting ready for this moment, and it is over before it ever even got started. What can you do? Nothing but do what Blyth is going to do...just keep going.

Probably the most exciting test of the day was the Frenchman, Didier Courreges. His horse was almost as wound up as Blyth's, but he came in and did what I would refer to as a typically French test. In other words, bordering on lunacy. While forward does not begin to describe it, he got away with it, and he deserved his score.

I am having quite a day. Olympic competition today, and tonight there will be a party in downtown Athens, with the three medal winners from Sydney in attendance. David O'Connor, Andrew Hoy, and Mark Todd make up a pretty good brain trust for the horse world. Plus there will be several other Olympic, World Championship, Pan Am, and European Championship medal winners in attendance. I have to make a short toast after dinner, and I have already written it out. "This is the greatest collection of horse talent since the last time Burt de Nemethy and Jack LeGoff had lunch together." It will be quite a gathering, and I am looking forward to it.

I have to drive into downtown Athens, which is not a job for the faint of heart, so I had better get going. More as it occurs to me.

AUGUST 16, 2004

Greetings from Athens. Picture this. Early morning at the Olympic training center. Quiet, a few early birds like me out and about, cool, clear skies with a promise of heat to come, but very comfortable right now. I had wandered alone up to the far training area to see if anything was going on yet. It is a good thing I did, because I had one of those moments that those of us who are horse crazy treasure for the rest of our lives.

I spotted a tall, elegant dressage rider in the far end of the arena, working in collected trot. It wasn't just the element of collection that drew my eye, but the unity, the harmony, the inner peace that defined the moment. When she turned towards me, I could see that it was Anky Von Gruesven. I had heard a great deal about her horse, Gestion Salinero, but had not seen it until now. As I watched, she turned up the long side and went into a passage-piaffe-passage series of transitions that were as good as I have ever seen. There is a lightness and elegance in her riding that defines dressage for me, and Salinero thinks he is playing with her, not working. She turned back to the other end of the arena, and did some suppling work, while I held my breath, and prayed the moment would continue.

The ring where she was working is at the top of a hill. Watching her, I was seeing her outlined against the top of the next mountain range. So when she turned down the long side of the arena, the early morning light brought a glow to the surroundings. The footing is so good in the training areas that the horses' footfalls are silent. And the angle of sight I had put the next ridge in the background at the level of her horses' feet. She repeated the same passage-piaffe-passage series again in the far corner, but this time she transformed it into the most powerful, correct, floating extended trot I have ever seen. I had the illusion that she was trotting across the tops of the mountain in the background, and her horses' steps were bounding from peak to peak.

That instant alone would be enough to make my trip worthwhile, but the moment got even better. Nearing the corner, she suddenly broke out into a beaming smile, gave a squeal of delight, dropped both reins, and slapped her horse on the neck, murmuring to him in approval and praise. He held his elevated frame for a few more steps, wagged his head back and forth as if to say, "Damn, we're good," smoothly lowered his head and neck at the trot, and went searching for grass along the edge of the ring, with Anky continuing to praise him. They walked by the out gate, and turned towards home, leaving me with a new definition of harmony in horsemanship.

I passed David O'Connor and Jane Savoie on my way out.

"Did you see that?" I asked.

"Oh, yeah," David said.

We smiled at each other, and just shook our heads. What can you say?

All of us had jobs for the day, so we went ahead, but we knew had seen something extraordinary.

In the past, competitors at a major event have consoled themselves after a disappointing dressage test with the thought, that "It's not a dressage contest, and the cross-country course will give me a chance to catch up." I don't think that is the case in a short-format event. I'm not alone in this belief. Most of the trainers I have spoken with feel the same way. This means there is more pressure on the dressage phase than ever, because if you fall behind now, you will never catch up. This was going through my mind as I watched the dressage tests today. I also felt a sense of relief that the wind was again blowing pretty hard, and affecting the outcome of the tests. I had been afraid last night that the wind would not be a factor today, thus producing two separate competitions. At least it is the same for everybody. We will have to wait until the final scores to come out, but from the looks on the faces of riders who were a little off in their dressage rides, they agree with me. If you are not in the top six or so of the dressage phase in a short format, you are not going to be waving at Mom on the 'Tron during the victory ceremony. It was a long day standing in the wind and sun, and as I trudged down the hill I couldn't help but think that I had had enough dressage for a while.

Some one recently asked me about the life I live these days, what with all the pressure, traveling, and time spent alone on the road. "It is not so bad," I said, "except that you have to go so many places they don't take Labradors." I have had a black Lab at my heel all my adult life, so I am like a man without a shadow right now.

Anyway the day is over, and the grounds were already quiet when I left. All the horses have finished their dressage, and have been put up for the night. The riders are still out walking the cross-country course, lonely figures trudging along, each one making their final plans, and going through their last minute rituals. The competition is in their hands now, and that's the way it should be. Tomorrow is a big day.

AUGUST 17, 2004

Greetings from Athens. The cross-country course turned out about as the insiders had expected, which is to say that it was easy for horses and riders at this level. It was funny talking about the course beforehand with my pals, as there was a conspiracy of silence about it. We all knew it was easy, but we were all afraid to say so, because that is considered terribly bad luck. Fortunately, we were right, as the alternative would have been a disaster for the sport. The real agenda for this competition is to stay on the Olympic calendar, and off the front pages of the newspapers. In my opinion, almost any compromise is acceptable to achieve that goal. We are fighting a holding action with the IOC, and indeed with our own international ruling body, which has been astonishingly and distressingly hostile to Eventing over the past Olympic quadrennial. This sort of day was the best possible outcome for our sport and I welcomed it. That doesn't mean I have changed my mind about the short format/long format controversy. There is no comparison...one is a test of training, and the other is the complete test of horse and rider. It is as simple as that.

I took a look at the jump fault sheets, and there were as many falls as refusals, which tells you that many of the riders were chasing the clock. (There were 13 refusals, and 13 falls, out of 75 starters. Only 3 involved the fall of a horse, and several of the falls of rider occurred when the horse refused to jump, and the rider fell off. Stupid *should* hurt.)

There will be a lot of discussion in the months to come about the rights and wrongs of the new format. It was designed by Germans for Germans and so on. At the same time, one of the German team's top three scores is held by a thoroughbred and one by an Irish Sport horse. I'll have to think about that one a little while.

The horses look pretty good, so all in all it was a satisfactory day for the sport.

Watching a major event these days is a bitter sweet experience for me. Have you ever heard of a bird called the Attwater's Prairie Chicken? There used to be millions of them, down in east Texas. They are beautiful, in an understated way, and have an elaborate mating dance, like most species. But the thing of it is that there are only 60 of them left, in an undisclosed location southwest of Houston. If you want to see one, you had better hurry, as they are only one prairie fire and a couple of coyote raids from extinction. My point being that if you destroy something's habitat, it goes away. And it doesn't come back. The website to learn more about Attwater is: http://www.earlham.edu/~stclaka/apchicken.htm

We need to think about the habitat of the things we love.

AUGUST 18, 2004

Greetings from Athens. There is no tension like that surrounding the final vet check at a big team competition. It is not that any-one wants to do away with the vet check; it is just that riders hate it when they can't affect the outcome. I thought the Ground Jury set a sensible standard. One coach murmured to a compatriot who was on his way to have his team inspected, "Don't worry; if they passed mine, they have *got* to pass yours!" Funny, but true enough. Some horses passed that were a little bit "knit-one-purl-two" but the lame horses were left in the stables.

The protocol at the final vet examination calls for the coach and the Chef D'Equipe to accompany the team when the horses are presented to the Ground Jury. You stand quietly at the end of the jogging lane, while your horses are inspected, as a recognition of your responsibility for the horses being presented. It is a brief moment of peace in an otherwise frantic atmosphere, and I always think of my father, who coached the U.S. team in 1952 at Helsinki. It is an odd feeling, to stand where he stood 52 years ago, but it gives me a sense of connection. I know he and Mom are watching. I hope they are enjoying the show.

I have been subsisting on a diet of cold cereal and hot dogs for the past 10 days, and my stomach is starting to mutiny. It was with a small sense of relief that I realized that I was putting away my last Greek hot dogs. There is probably stuff in there that eats Salmonella for breakfast. At least in the States, they don't lie to you on the label: "Pork hearts and beef by-products."

At this point it is a blessing that I don't read Greek. What would these labels say: "Road kill and octopus by-product"?

I don't wanna think about it. If you are what you eat, I'm going to glow in the dark by the time I get back to the States.

I'm getting ahead of the story, but did you notice there was no one in the grandstand for the final show jumping? No, all the seats were sold out. What happened is that about mid-afternoon the food vendors at Marcopoulo Stadium got a surprise visit from...are you ready?...drum roll!...yup, the Ministry of Food and Health. Shut those suckers right down. So, people did the understandable thing, and said, "We can have some fried squid at that lovely little spot on the beach at Porto Ransi, and catch the final on the boob tube." Hence, no crowd. Remember that old definition of an honest politician? When he is bought, he stays bought! Major bribery breakdown here, if you ask me.

I'm not saying they shouldn't have been shut down. Modern society disapproves of serving underage rats. It is just that their sense of timing was a little off.

One last word about the attitude behind the scenes here in Athens. The stewards have been nothing short of terrific throughout the Games. Remember those exercise rings I mentioned earlier? They have at least one steward on duty at all times. The stewards are there ostensibly to enforce the FEI and IOC rules, and at past Games they have been a major irritant...officious, pedantic, and bureaucratic. Here, they have been just the reverse.

I was warming up Mike Winter for the team round of show jumping. His horse, Ballista, is a thoroughbred, and gets pretty competitive in front of crowds. There was a long walk from the final warm-up to the main arena, under a tunnel and down a ramp. Because everyone is nervous, not just the riders and coaches, they had been sending the horses down quite early, and making the horse wait next to the railing of the main arena. I came over to the two young ladies at the gate who were sending the horses down according to the order of go, and asked for a little more time before they sent Ballista down to wait his turn.

"Don't worry, no problem," was the reply. At this point one of the young ladies' radio started giving off, with the man on the other end obviously in a condition. She spoke soothingly into it, turned to me, and smiled. "I told the chief steward you had already started down," she said, "but you can take another minute or so before you really have to go. We will let you know." At the last possible instant she sent us down the ramp. I thanked her profusely as I went by. "Don't worry," she said again, and turned to look for the next horse. That has been the attitude throughout, of caring for the horses and riders, not enforcing the timetable.

I know, I know, you want to cut to the chase and start talking about Horsegate, but we need to talk about the show jumping courses first. I thought the designer, Olaf Peterson, did an excellent job with both the team and the individual courses. They were not huge, but technical, and very airy. The oxers were square, and the verticals did not have any ground lines, so you had to be accurate, and your horse had to want to leave the jumps up. Probably the biggest crowd pleaser was Amy Tryon, who jumped one of only two double-clear rounds to move up to 7th from 22nd after the cross-country. Poggio has never exactly been what you might call disciplined, and the pressure of the Olympics brought out the best (or worst, if you are Mark Phillips and George Morris, writhing with fear on the sidelines) in him. Amy would make a smooth, balanced turn, look for her stride to the next jump, and Poggio would chuck his head, and take off like a scalded cat for it. After a desultory, half-hearted half-halt, Amy would put her hands down and let him sort it out. Twenty-eight efforts spread over two rounds, and all of them stayed up, somehow.

"I figured if I just let him tear around like I do cross-country, he'd figure it out," Amy said. Nerve wracking, but it worked. George Morris, the U.S. Eventing team show jumping guru, did not look as if he were listening to celestial music as she was going around, but what can I say? The jumps stayed up.

Unfortunately, they did not all stay up for Kim Severson. It tells you something about her talent, when I say that I am disappointed that she got the Bronze. I was convinced she was going to win it. But the margin at this level is incredibly small. My Canadian team was only two-tenths of a point behind the next team. That works out to one rider getting one mark better on his position from one dressage judge, over three days!

I saw Kim right after the medal ceremony, and she was being the best possible sport about the results, but I know her well enough to see that she was tormented inside. She blames herself for the U.S. team's failure to win a medal. That is not how it works, but that is the way the great ones think, and that's what she is dealing with right now. Do you listen to John Mayer? Check him out. Good voice, good musician, and fabulous song writer. He has a song called "No Such Thing." Some of the lyrics go:

"I'd like to think the best of me is still hidden, up my sleeve."

Kim is painfully shy, and she keeps most of what she thinks up her sleeve. But one of these days she will reach up her sleeve and pull out a handful of Gold medals, and she will redefine excellence when she does it.

We have always been fortunate in the people we have at the top of our sport, and Bettina Hoy, from Germany, is no exception. There is no one alive less deserving of the turmoil that surrounded (and continues to surround, as of this writing) the final result. She is an absolutely admirable person, as well as being a worthy medal winner.

I don't know if you saw it on TV, but there was a moment when Bettina came out of the ring after the medal ceremony, which by now was being held under protest, a protest that would later take the gold medal away from her. She jumped down and hugged her husband, the Australian three-time Gold medal winner, Andrew Hoy. They clung to each other for an instant, then turned, faced the cameras, and smiled and waved. Two things occurred to me simultaneously: one was that the Hoys have just supplanted the O'Connors as the Eventing partnership of the century; and two, that Bettina's and Andrew's smiles were strained, and the lines around their eyes were deeper, and they seemed to be leaning against each other, as if bracing for the winds of controversy they know are sure to follow. No one deserves it less, but no one is better equipped to handle whatever comes with poise and grace.

All you can say about the situation is that there are not going to be any winners, only losers. Whatever happens, there will always be an asterisk next to the results in the history books. At the same time, you can't be too judgmental of the British, French, and U.S. teams for protesting. This is a big business these days, and all three teams receive money from their governments and Olympic committees. They owe it to their employers to leave no stone unturned. My own opinion? I was sitting there, but did not notice it, and haven't seen the tapes. It is too late for all that anyway, as this sort of thing has a momentum all its own. We are just riding shotgun down the avalanche.

So it will go to arbitration, and whatever happens happens. All I can tell you is that when I left the stadium, I happened to catch up with Bettina's horse, Ringwood Cockatoo. His groom was alternately crying with joy and chatting excitedly with her pals. She did not notice an old, broken down ex-eventer step in next to her lovely grey, murmur a couple of words into his ear, and give him a reverent pat on the neck. He turned to see who it was, and I could see the Irish sense of humor in his eye, so typical of his type. It was obvious to me that he thinks he is pretty special. I think so, too. I gave him one more pat, and walked on alone, down the hill into the dark. I thought of my late friend, Reiner Klimke. He had a saying that sums up the whole situation for me. He used to say: "My horses are not my slaves. They are my friends."

"With a friend like that," I thought, "Bettina doesn't have to worry about how it comes out."

I'm pretty tired, and homesick, and I am headed back to the Blue Ridge. It is a long way from Milford, Kansas, but the Blue Ridge is home now. I have three grandsons that I haven't seen for a while, a Lab who misses me, and a wife who just put my picture on a milk carton. I hope you enjoyed reading my diary as much as I did living through it. Give your four-legged friend a pat for me...that's what it is all about. Goodbye from Athens.

GREETINGS
FROM AACHEN*

I have been doing work for television off and on most of my life, so when NBC called me about doing the color commentary for the World Championships in Aachen, Germany, I was ready. Working behind the scenes for TV is the best seat in the house. You get a chance to soak up the atmosphere, plus watch the shots from all the cameras while they are showing the various competitions.

Then I thought, "What the heck I'm going to be there any way, I wonder if I can find anybody to carry another one of my weblogs?" So I called Cathy Laws, at Primedia, and caught her in a weak moment. Primedia already sort of puts up with me, as they are the publishers of Practical Horseman, where I do a monthly column.) I told Cathy that

*Reprinted by permission of equisearch.com

I understood that Primedia is a G-rated website and that promised I would keep the material within bounds. Obviously, I lied, and I got into a little trouble about it...all I can say is that you should see the stuff I left out! Besides, anybody that watches "Triumph the Insult Comic Dog" from Late Night with Conan O'Brien *has had their consciousness raised (or lowered) when it comes to setting the boundaries. But more about Triumph later...*

AUGUST 23, 2006

Greetings from Aachen. I am here in Germany for the World Championships and will post some of my impressions as the week goes along. Let's get the disclaimer out of the way right away...if you want the straight truth, you have come to the wrong place. If you want to know what the *Real* story is, then OK, we've got a deal. I make this comparison all the time, about that guy who worked for Bill Clinton testifying under oath that he had lied to his diary. So I am going to keep a sorta Bill Clinton diary. If it didn't happen the way I tell it, it should have!

My real reason for being over here is that I am doing the commentary for NBC, so I will have the best seat in the house. If you really want to see a big time horse event these days, the way to do it is to wrangle your way into the production truck. That is where all the various cameras show their pictures in real time, so you are not just watching what will finally be shown to the TV audience, but the rest of the pictures as well. (By the way, this program will air at 4:30-6:00 p.m. Eastern Standard Time on Sunday the 24th of September on the main NBC channel. Shameless plug.)

This is a real trip down memory lane for me, as the last time I was in Aachen was in 1956, when my brother Warren was riding here. The grounds are the same as then, but not really. There are four big, enclosed grandstands around the arena now, and the trade fair is way larger, but the smell of the rostbratwurst is the same, and the anticipation on the faces of the crowd.

Rolex smells different, and looks different, but the underlying excitement and sense of occasion is the same, because you know that when you come here you are going to see something special.

Aachen looks special these days, which is a change from the last time I saw it, when it was still digging out of the rubble of World War Two. Young boys are fascinated by burned out buildings and walls with bullet holes all over them, and it wasn't until years later that I took into account the devastation that I was witness to at the time.

My family really made a trip of it in 1956, going to a lot of the horse shows here in Germany. I remember Hamburg, Düsseldorf, Cologne, and of course, Aachen. All of those cities were pretty much in the same shape that year...there wasn't much left of your town after Georgie Patton and the third Army got through with it. Of course all that went over my little 10-year old red head.

The thing I remember the most from that trip is dipping tadpoles out of one of the water jumps in the Hamburg Derby arena, sneaking them back to the Hamburger Hof, and putting them in the ornamental fountain in the main dining room. I woulda gotten away with it, too, but the darned things hatched out and started croaking like mad. So I did the only thing I could think of at the time...I blamed it on young Johnny Russell.

Anyway, we were speaking of special, and it doesn't get any more special than the World Championships. People have worked most of their lives to get here and some of the riders are walking around looking like they just saw Elvis walk out of the mother ship...carrying Tom Cruise's baby. But that won't last as the competition has already started with a bang.

Endurance was held this past weekend in rain and deep mud, and there were some tired puppies out there. The U.S. team covered themselves with mud, but no glory. Many of the endurance horses have already shipped out, and they aren't sorry to leave as their stable area has been flooded for the last three days, with water running through the aisles and into the stalls. Needless to say, they were a little grumpy, but the organizing committee has been spreading sand like mad, and digging ditches, and generally trying to take care of the situation.

This is the sixth World Championship I have been to as either a rider, coach, spectator, or now TV commentator, and every organizing committee I have ever watched has thought they had things under control going into it, only to watch things get all *upgefuchen* (that's German for "gosh, what a mess") at the last minute. I heard a rumor that the stable manager finally told one especially waspish Chef-de-Equipe to click her heels together three times and go screw herself, but that is probably only a rumor.

So far, the Germans are taking the same approach they did in Munich during the 1972 Olympics. They are so determined to put the Nazi stereotype to bed that they are bending over backwards to make sure everyone feels welcome...except for that cop this morning, but what the heck, it was a one-way street after all. Huh? Oh, for sure the other way. What can I say? Rules were meant to be broken.

Despite that unscheduled detour, I got here this afternoon just in time to watch the U.S. Dressage team get their Bronze medals, which is good news for a group that has really been digging down and working for success. The look of pride on Klaus Balkenhol's face was a study, and several of the U.S. dressage groupies in the stands were having a Kleenex moment. Can't say I blame them.

The U.S. Eventing team all passed the vet check today, as did all the rest of the horses that were presented, and their first day of competition starts tomorrow morning. Andrew Hoy had a scare with Master Monarch, as he was held for reinspection but got through on the second attempt. That can't have done his nerves any good, but he is too old a hand to let that put him off his game.

I usually stick my neck out and try to predict the winners, but I won't do that yet, as I want to see the horses and walk the cross-country course before I get that brave. I'll post my impressions of the course tomorrow, but my jet lag is kicking in now, so I am going to reach down into my carry-on (yes, my carry-on, you didn't think my luggage would make it, did you?) and pull out this all-purpose brown fluid. The label says "Caution—after drinking this, you will self-destruct in three...two...one..."

August 24, 2006

Greetings from Aachen. I know you are following the results on the Internet, so I won't bother much with the placings. But you know you are at the World Championships when riders from three different countries stop you and say, "Wasn't that too bad about the British rider, blowing up in the dressage ring like that?" And all the time you can hear them thinking, "Oh, yeah, I'm in with a chance!" They will worry about the human cost next week, but for now, someone else's misfortune in an opportunity for them. It is a tough world here, and we are at the World Championships, right?

By now I would have flunked out of the Journalist's World Championships, for forgetting to tell you yesterday that one of the Irish horses was eliminated at the first vet check, and the one with the best name in all of eventing, too, Drunken Disorderly. His rider, Mark Kyle, will be the life of the party for sure...he's got nothing else to do for the rest of the week. Bummer, dude.

The rain that was in the forecast has held off so far, which is a good thing if you like Scandinavian type girls. The ladies cross the line from erotic to prurient in a hurry over here, so I am praying for sunshine the next couple of days. No telling what some of these Britney Spears wannabes will show up wearing (or not wearing) tomorrow. I'm keeping a list of the pick-up lines I have heard in the bar, and I'll share them with you later, but I know you would rather talk about dressage right now, not those hussies walking around looking like an eight-ounce muffin in a four-ounce cup.

So far, the dressage is not as good as I had thought it would be. There is not a lot of atmosphere in the arena, and the stands are only about half full, but most of the riders are riding a little tight. There has been some rumbling behind the scenes that the footing is a little slick and so on, but my own experience is that nervous riders get tight and make their horses slip, and aggressive riders go forward and make their horses stick their feet deeper in to the turf. Phillip Dutton came in this afternoon on Connaught, and never slipped a bit. Of course, he was most definitely going for every point out there, and his score showed it. There are some good horses still to come, so we have not seen the best of it yet.

They have done a good job of putting things close together here. The main stadium is right next to the eventing and the third arena, where the vaulting and reining will take place, is just beyond that, while the cross country course is right across the street. Cute story about vaulting: One of our vaulting team is only 10 years old, about four-foot nothing, and maybe 50 pounds in wet spandex. So she comes up to Jim Wolf, who is in charge of all the disciplines here, and says "Mr. Wolf, can you ask them if they can raise the roof here in the stadium?" You need to know that the bleachers and ring are permanent, but the roof has been put in especially so that the vaulting and reining don't have to worry about the weather. So Wolf goes off to the nightly Chef du Mission's meeting last night and asks them to raise the roof, because our vaulters are so strong, and getting so much loft in their tosses that they are going to hit the ceiling otherwise.

Welcome to the 21st Century, where even 10-year-olds know how to talk trash and get inside their competitor's heads. It is working so far...last I heard we were in the lead for the vaulting compulsories!

I had a chance to get out and look at the cross-country course, and nobody feels like they are wasting their time here. It is big overall, and technical in places. Every course has its own feel, and this has a very country, natural feel, even though it is on the outskirts of Aachen. It is on a working farm, so as you walk out to the start, you go past several paddocks full of horses that trot up and down just beyond the electric wire, obviously enjoying the company and all the buzz from the other side of the street. The dairy cows in the barnyard don't pay any attention, as they are too busy chowing down on the fresh silage that has overwhelmed your olfactory nerves by now. That stuff is strong over here! It is probably a good thing I did not bring my Labrador,

Nacho, over here. He would have been on those barnyard ducks like Martha Stewart's parole bracelet, and the Organizing Committee would have airmailed both of us outta here by now.

They have obviously gone to a lot of trouble with the cross-country course. The galloping track is grass, but it has been graded, reseeded, rolled, aerovated, and otherwise been primped within an inch of its life. I couldn't help but think when I saw all the work that has gone into things here that one of these upper-level courses is kind of like K-Y jelly...not many other uses for it. I know, I know, I'm a sick man. (Cue insane laughter sound track here.) Keep reading, I promise to behave.

The course starts out with the usual big, easy galloping fences, and the first real problem come at #4 and #5, which are big offset hedges. The white flag of #4 barely overlaps the red flag at #5, so your horse has to hold a severe right-to-left angle here; but these horses handle stuff like this every day, so there should not be much trouble. After this, you gallop across the road into the main park where you cut through the Eventing arena and jump #6 and #7, two big tables, on a sweeping right-hand curve. You immediately leave the main park back across the same road. The course will come back this way later on, so between #7 and #8 you gallop over a bridge with a tunnel underneath it. The bridge takes you to #8, and later on the tunnel will take you to #30 and #31. Stay with me here.

The course runs slightly downhill to the coffin at #8ABC. They call it the "Soers Canyon" for the name of the farm here, Soers. There is a big log with a good-sized drop, quite a forward stride to a big ditch, then two strides up to another log at C. It is big, but again these horses won't think much of it.

The jumps at #9, #10, and 11 are quite big, but straightforward. The first water complex is #12ABCD, the "Seaside Resort Soers." You jump a cabin at a slight left-to-right angle, take four strides and jump a 3'6" rail down into water. The drop here is maximum, at 6'6" and the water is probably 14 inches deep, so there will be a considerable feeling of "welcome to the National Football League" when you land. You don't have time to think about things since you need to keep your horse on his line, take four strides, jump up a big bank out of the water, take one stride, jump a narrow cabin on top of the mound in the water, gallop down a ramp back into the water, back on dry land, and finally jump a narrow fence at #13. None of these obstacles at #12 and #13 are extraordinary in themselves, but they are hard, even by World Championship standards, and there is a lot going on in a short space of time, so I expect the first serious problems to happen here. I suppose there might be the odd refusal before that, but pressure makes riders do dumb things, and you can't fix stupid.

After this, you swing uphill, and the course becomes physical for the first time. You are going to be climbing uphill for the next 800 meters, and the jumps will start to take their toll. The Hay Rack at #14 is big and slightly uphill, but easy. The Normandy Bank at #15ABC, is very big, and the space between the ditch-and-upbank at A, and the narrow log at B is built for a short bounce. You need a Goldilocks pace here...not too fast, not too slow, but just right. Too slow, and you can't get up the 3'9" bank with a 6' ditch. Too fast, and you will carry too far into the bounce before the narrow log and have a stop, or worse. The narrow log at #15C comes up quickly, and if you are patting yourself on the back when you jump A and B, you will be kicking yourself if you don't pay attention to the last fence here.

The climb becomes steeper at this point, and the Bullfinch at #16 will ride very big, but you should be going at a racing pace and good horses won't be bothered. The Produce Stand at #17 is big and gorgeous, but should not be influential. If you have ever been here, you know that this is the highest point on the course; and when you look back, you realize you have been galloping uphill fast and jumping big fences for a couple of minutes straight...if you know what you are doing, you will give your horse a breather here.

The Fallen Tree at #18 is a trap for the unwary. You have turned downhill after #17 and are picking up the pace, but the ground falls away over your horse's left shoulder. You will have to deal with a light-to-shade problem, and there is a bit more of a right-handed turn needed to get ready for the narrow opening than some might assume. One or two riders will regret this fence—after they run past it the first time, but experience is what you get right after you needed it.

The Hedges and Corners at #19AB are quite a test of accuracy. You jump a maximum hedge (4'7") at a slight right-to-left angle at A, take five strides, and then jump a white flag corner at B on a right-to-left angle, which is exactly what you don't want to do at a white flag corner. If your horse is not straight and honest here, your weiner is schnitzeled. I haven't made too much of a thing about it, but all the complexes have long routes through them. Most of the riders will ignore them, as they are very long, and involve a lot of twisting and turning.

After the Hedges and Corner, you take six strides, and jump a log at #20. It is a plain fence, but the ground falls away in a sneaky fashion, and you need to be careful with this one, as you are going to get there a bit sooner than you might expect.

You then have a long run over to #21, the Trakehner, and then around a turn, and slightly uphill to the Sunken Meadow, #22ABCD. This involves 3'6" rails, one stride, down a 3'9" drop into a sunken road, one short stride to a 3'6" wall, then two forward strides to a brush box at D that is 3'6" high, 6'6" spread, but only a 4' face on it. This is like the Sunken Road at Rolex this year, but on steroids.

The second water complex is at #23, the Eifel Village. This is a pretty simple jump, just a table in the water. But remember the first water at #12 and #13? The question there was first of all, to jump from dry land to water...then water to dry land, then gallop into and out water and jump. Now at #23, you are asked to jump from water to water. Remember this, because you have another water jump to go later on, and the question will be different still. But I don't want to get ahead of myself, and I'll come back to this in my summary.

After #23, there is very big hedge at #24. The landing is level, but you are going uphill until you get to it, so your horse has to be brave as well as scopey here, since he can't see the landing until he takes off. You land, take two strides, jump an identical hedge at #25A, then run downhill and jump a red flag corner, #25B, on an extreme left-to-right angle. This is a mirror image of the problem you dealt with at the Hedges and Corner, #19AB. The problem back then was to hold a right-to-left line, and now here at #24 and #25AB, the question is to hold a left-to-right line. Note the mirror image problems that the course designer, Rudiger Schwarz, is posing through out the course. You will hear more about that in a minute.

The Countryside View is a simple table at #26, and then you turn downhill back towards home for the last time. The third water complex at #27 is the only place where I think the course designer might have crossed over the line a bit. There is an extreme right-to-left angle over a 3'9" wall, landing on a down slope to a 3'10" rolltop into water. Note that a different question is asked of the horses here, to jump and land on dry land with water in view, take a stride, then land in the water, gallop and turn, come back onto dry land, curve left on a six stride line, and finish over a big rolltop at #27C. If I had to get through this complex, I would probably go the long way in, which involves an extra turn, but does not carry the risk I feel when contemplating the fast route.

I caught up with Lucinda Green at this point when I was walking around, and she had much the same opinion as I did, that it might just be that little bit too hard. When I walked on, she was still parked in front of the fast line, with a very sour look on her face. I hope I am wrong, but the medals may very well be won and lost here.

No matter what happens, you have to gallop on towards the finish line. The course crosses under itself here by the simple means of going through a tunnel. You galloped over it on your way to #6, and now you pop out of the tunnel, to find #29, the Water Trough, just after a left handed turn. Remember those mirror image problems I mentioned earlier? Remember #18, where the course curved downhill to the right, with a narrow-faced jump, and a light-to-dark factor. Well, here you go...the exact problem, but in the other direction, and two miles later on into the course. Here at #29, you deal with the light to dark first, as you come out of the tunnel, then a turn to the left, which will be sharper than it walks because your horse is tired now and a little sluggish in his steering, and the jump is just that little bit more narrow than you remember it was, and you are in a hurry because you have a chance to make the time at the World Championships and…"Damn! How'd I miss that dang thing?" Winners have medals, and losers have excuses. The last two fences, #30 and #31 are fly fences, and should pose no problem if you have gotten this far.

So what do I think overall? I think the same thing that I did this spring when I walked Rolex. This course is big, and it is hard, and it is going to get harder as you go along. There are several reasons for this. First of all, modern cross-country course design is frozen right now. There have not been any new developments in design for the past eight or ten years. The main reason for this is the ever-increasing emphasis on safety. If a designer tries something new or different, and it doesn't work, he gets run out of town on a rail. Look at what happened to Mike Tucker, the designer at the 2002 World Games in Jerez, Spain. He designed a very big, old-fashioned, square course, which took judgment, skill, and a sober attitude towards the time and speed element. What happened? The riders all tried to make the time, turned their horse over, and blamed the course designer for their shortcomings! I don't blame the designers for being conservative at all. If I were still designing courses, I would be doing the same thing.

But the result is when riders walk a course, they are seeing the same sort of fence that they have seen all spring and summer. Familiarity in this context doesn't exactly breed contempt, but it does lead to a certain amount of complacency, an "oh, yeah, that fence is just like the so-and-so at Badminton" sort of thing. Thus, riders tend to forget that while a problem is obvious, that doesn't mean it is no longer a problem. You still have to provide the right answer.

In addition, the new short format is not the slam dunk that some of the riders thought it would be. We have merely exchanged one kind of stress for another. It is ironic that the Germans, who were behind the movement to change to the short format, are now scratching their heads and saying *"Gottfordammerung"* or whatever it is that they say when they get what they asked for, but it isn't what they wanted. Some of the German riders are having some success right now, but they are doing it on Thoroughbreds and Irish sport horses, not old-fashioned warmbloods.

Again, the emphasis on safety has led designers to use complicated complexes to try and slow the riders down. This works for as long as it takes for the riders to jump the complex, but then the riders sprint away from this complex, because they know they are behind the clock, and they have to make up time on their way to the next complex, and so on and so on—to fatigue on the horse's part. By this time, these complexes start to get too complex for the average world class horse, if there is such a creature, and, well, you start to see things come unraveled. We saw the process at Rolex, and I think we will see the same thing here. I would predict that the entire field will jump the first 10 fences clean, and then the penalties will increase geometrically as we go along in the course.

Finally, this course is hard because it is designed to be hard. It is a very subtle course in many ways, with the endless repetition of mirror image questions, and minor details that are suddenly not so minor when you are going too fast on a tired horse. The one thing you can be sure of is that if your horse has a hole in his education anywhere, this course will search it out and expose it.

Don't get me wrong, I think there will be plenty of clear rounds, and if we don't get any more rain (don't forget those Britney Spears wannabes...I haven't!) there should be between seven and ten clear rounds inside the time. But if it rains, like Keb' Mo' says "thass a 'hole 'nother thing!" This is new turf, and it won't hold up to heavy traffic.

Just as an aside, this is yet another reason that I disagree with the current trend towards making courses more and more narrow: when you have heavy rain, you no longer have a level playing field, because a narrow fence forces every horse to jump off the same piece of ground. If it gets muddy, this is an obvious disadvantage to the horses that go late in the day.

Anyway, life ain't fair, so you gotta get over it, and get on with it. Friday is just around the corner, and I have to look into my crystal ball to see whom I think the winning teams and individuals will be. I am cheating a little, as by then I will know what the dressage scores are, but you gotta take every chance you get. In the meantime, I need to take me some of that all-purpose brown nerve tonic and get on with it. Have a good night, and I'll talk to you tomorrow.

BTW (that's computer talk for "by the way"...pretty cutting edge, huh?), if my luggage ever gets here, and I am not too computer-challenged, I will try to post some photos of the cross-country course tomorrow...but no promises. When that nerve tonic gets in your eye, there is no telling what happens next!

AUGUST 25, 2006

Greetings from Aachen. Boy, when you get lost around here, you can really get lost. We missed one exit off the Autobahn, and the next thing we knew, we were lost in three languages...four, if you count English. We went through the Netherlands and Belgium before we got back to Germany, and it only took 20 minutes. When the big guy in a *Politzei* uniform gets off his BMW motorcycle and comes over and says, "Yah, vot can I help you?" that is the German redneck version of "Ya'll ain't from 'round heah, are ya?"

"Yup" I said "the only thing more lost than me is my luggage." He didn't get it. Anyway, no harm, no foul.

We have got it a lot easier than the rest of the international media, who are depending on the Organizing Committee's shuttle system to get them around. This is great, but the shuttle picks them up and drops them off at different places every day, at a time to be determined in the future. Needless to say, The Press (notice the caps) is not happy. You want to get a tongue-lashing, drop off a photographer with bad feet, a 500-mm lens, and a 30-pound knapsack a mile out of their way. It gets ugly in a hurry.

Talk about ugly, I am in the *scheisse* around here. (That's German for deep macaca.) Yesterday, I forgot this site is G-rated.

Hoo boy, I need hip boots for the macaca I am in...no, I'm not going to tell you what I said, you think I'm crazy? If I tell you, you don't have to read it, and you are supposed to read it, or EquiSearch is going to be mad at me twice. John Ashcroft ain't gonna have to email me again, no siree bob.

What this really is, is a G-rated website for horse lovers, and you would feel right at home here in Aachen. The stands for the Grand Prix Dressage are packed (25,000–30,000), they clap in rhythm with the horse as he trots out after his test, and they gasp if the horse skips a beat in one of the piaffe sequences. These guys know what they are watching.

During the lunch break they had a display of German stallions, and it sounded like they were having a rock concert. The fans are not just confined to the stands either. Aachen's town square is next to the cathedral, and there is a stage set up, where a Jumbotron is showing live action all day long. People are sitting under umbrellas, drinking a beer, and watching dressage for fun. Go figure.

The Eventing Dressage is better today, and both Bettina Hoy and Zara Phillips lit up the world with their tests. I'll get to my picks in a minute, but you can take a hint. Besides the stallions, there was a display in the Eventing arena this afternoon. This place is a literal three-ring circus...the reining and vaulters have a stadium to themselves. At one point today, all three stadiums were going at once, and there was always a wave of applause washing over the grounds. I caught the vaulters act earlier today. Holy cow...these guys do stuff on purpose that I spent years doing by accident. And they land on their feet, too.

During the lunch break, 10 local German pony clubbers did a quadrille ride in the Eventing arena. All 10 horses were on the bit, and all of the kids had a position to die for...they know how to sit over here. We would have to search the entire country to get ten kids that could sit and ride like that, and these were just local pony club kids. Makes you worry, and understand why the Germans are such a powerhouse.

They showed their power in the Grand Prix, and Isabelle Werth really had the place going with Satchmo. The stands here are concrete...the last time I saw concrete stands rocking like that, it was at RFK Stadium, and the Redskins had come back in the fourth quarter to beat the Cowboys and advance to the play-offs. But that had nothing on the main arena here at Aachen. Anky von Grusven's horse, Salinero, is a favorite of mine, but he didn't quite have it today. Anky was smiling and waving on the silver medal stand, but her smile did not get all the way to her eyes, and I would bet that mentally she was already planning her training schedule for the Beijing Olympics in 2008. Andreas Helgstrand from Denmark lived up to his advance billing, and the U.S.A.'s Stefan Peters should be proud...fourth place in this company is better than a dry hacking cough, for sure.

It is starting to drizzle a slow, soft, steady drizzle, and there are some long faces in the eventing barns. The footing on the course is good, but can't take too much more rain or it will start to affect the outcome. Fingers crossed.

So, about that outcome...well, I dunno what to tell you. Based on their scores so far, Bettina and Zara have the inside track, followed by Andreas Dibowski and Kim Severson. I am not a betting man, but if I were, I would bet that when the dust settles (or the mud dries out) it will be Gold—Kim Severson, Silver—Andrew Hoy, and Bronze—Zara Phillips. The teams will be Great Britain, U.S.A., and Germany in that order. My wild cards would be Clayton Fredericks, Karin Donckers, and Nicolas Touzaint, and my wild card team would be the French.

The obvious ones left off my list are William Fox-Pitt, Ingrid Klimke, and Bettina Hoy. I love William's riding, but he is not lucky, and Napoleon thought that was the most important attribute a man could have, to be lucky. I hope his luck turns here. He deserves it. Ingrid had a heck of a fall a couple of weeks ago, rang her bell pretty thoroughly, and the jury is still out on her. And Bettina? Well, Bettina got convicted of RWB (riding while blonde) at Athens, and I don't think she will shake the hex here. I'm sticking pins in a miniature start line on the course map like mad, because she is a lovely person, but I don't think it will help.

It has been a long road to Aachen for all these kids, and there are a lot of broken hearts left behind. In January everyone could see themselves on the medal stand, but along the way something went wrong, and there are only these few horses and riders left, and only one of them will be the World Champion.

Muhammad Ali said champions have to have last minute stamina, and that they have to have both skill and will, but that the will must be stronger than the skill. They will need that stamina in the last minute over this course, and they must have that rock-solid, unshakable confidence in themselves and their horse. We have got it easy; all we have to do is sit back and watch. The horses and riders are in charge now. They wouldn't have it any other way.

As for me, when I lift the first one tonight, I'll drink a little toast to the horses. They are the reason I'm here.

AUGUST 26, 2006

Greetings from Aachen. They do it every time. Just when you learn the traffic pattern, they change it. We got to the grounds early this morning to find that none of the TV crews could get onto the grounds with their trucks and equipment. The gates we usually used are suddenly part of the galloping track for the cross-country. No worries...we disassembled part of the security fence, cut our way into the compound, and were on the air before security figured out we were not part of the grounds crew. They yelled at us for a minute, but we smiled, waved, and said have a nice day in English. I don't care what your mother says, sometimes it helps not to understand a second language.

We were a little foggy anyway, as last night we had stayed late here at the production truck. When we finally closed up shop for the night, we wandered down the main street of the show grounds and found there has been a major party going on every night. Rock bands, disco lights, champagne bars next to the sushi, next to the crepes, next to the pizza next to the beer garden, and all of them packed. We grabbed some eminently forgettable grub, had some local beer, and finally called it a night.

We did notice that the girls here are [*WARNING—contains deleted material; The Net Nanny is watching*]

We are getting kind of punchy now, as the hours are long and the meals are irregular, so I want to share something we think is hysterical: So this English boat goes on the radio and says "I say, my good chap, Mayday, Mayday, we are sinking!" We are sinking! And the German Coast Guard comes back and says, "Vot are you sinking about?"

Ahh, you had to be there.

You know all about the results by now, so I can go to the color commentary. The first thing I noticed is how fast things can come unraveled at this level. It doesn't matter how much experience you have either...if you snooze, you lose. The list of people this course bit in the [*This is your last warning—The Net Nanny*] reads like a who's who of the horse world. Take it from the top:

Jean Teulure–2002 World Champion

Andrew Hoy–has two legs on the Rolex Grand Slam

Kim Severson–three-time winner at Rolex, Individual Olympic Silver, team Gold 2002 WEG etc., etc., etc.

Karen O'Connor–multiple medals, multiple Rolex

Ingrid Klimke–Second at Badminton 2006

Andrew Nicholson–maybe the best athlete in the saddle in the world

Phillip Dutton–see above

William Fox Pitt–ah, but is he lucky?

When you look at this list, you would not have bet that all of them would have a glance-off today. None of them fell, none of them had a really bad fence, they just...missed.

And the margin that they missed by is so heart breakingly small that I promise you they are all thinking right now. "How did that happen? All I did was ((insert excuse)) for a split second and the next thing I knew, I was past the flag!" Muhammad Ali sure knows a thing or something, when he says the will must be stronger than the skill. There was a big gap between riders seeing their stride and riders making that stride happen. What's that line I use? There are riders that make it happen, there are riders that watch it happen, and there are a riders who wonder "what happened?" There was a lot of number three going on today.

On the other hand, I saw some neat stuff. I love good riding, and I don't much care where they come from...horse lovers don't look at the flag on your saddlecloth. Zara Phillips deserves her place right now, on top of the world...she made a couple of rookie mistakes, but she has a fabulous horse, and Toy Town gets it, and was there for her when she needed him.

If you hang around this sport long enough, some times the eventing gods pat you on the head, and say, "Here, kid, we're going to make up to you for all the bad feng shui you have had to deal with for all these years. You never gave up, and you never quit, so Bettina, we are gonna give you another chance. Don't blow it this time!" I hope she doesn't.

Second chances don't usually happen in sport, or in life for that matter. I went into the show jumping arena in the 1968 Mexico Olympics with a chance at an individual Gold medal. I slipped, fell on a turn, and wound up sixth. It was a long time before my second chance came. But during that long time, I made sure that I never, but never, ever took anything for granted.

We have taken some of our great riders for granted, and they won't be operating at this level for much longer, so you need to watch them when you get the chance...their window of opportunity is closing.

Who else caught my eye? Clayton Fredericks, for sure. He's been knocking on the door for a while now, and he blew their doors off today. He rides in a lovely rhythm, and his horse gets to the jumps in balance and in a good package.

I have never seen Sharon Hunt ride before, and it was a treat today. She thinks under pressure and is a nice mixture of modern accuracy and old-fashioned git-'er-done. She also is the first rider I have seen since the legendary Lucinda Green who understands the art of showing the whip without using the whip. Sweet piece of riding, Sharon.

Joe Meyer, from New Zealand, is no Blyth Tait yet, but he is the same shape of rider, and he gets it. Who else?

Daisy Dick, from England, is a good new rider at this level. Her eye still gets longer than her stride, but I'll take that over some putz who goes down to a jump with hands like the Texas Chainsaw Massacre. Some horse, too.

You probably won't see him again, as he comes from Poland, and they don't have much in the way of owners there, or big time eventing, but this kid has the stuff...at the start of World War II, in September of 1939, the Polish Cavalry defending Warsaw charged German Panzer tanks armed only with lances. I'll bet his grandfather was involved. Brave kid, with a future in the sport, if he can seize it. My pick for the "Who-dat" award would be Pawel Spisak. Don't get me wrong, Pawel stunk up the joint today, but that's what rookies do. He'll get over it. His horse isn't worth the powder to blow him up, but I'm just sayin'...

It was a good day for the sport. The weather cooperated, the footing held up, the course got a good result without being punishing (only three horse falls, I think, plus a couple more involuntary flying dismounts), and the jump penalties were spread out around the course. A big crowd was on hand, and they are still having a good time...I can hear them rocking the show grounds behind the production truck as I finish today's section. *Haben sie ein bier, bitte?* See, if I drink enough scotch, English is my second language.

AUGUST 27, 2006

Greetings from Aachen. I have been writing this blog sitting in the back of the TV production truck. I put on my head phones, turn the volume up, and crank up my tunes to get in the right mood for contact journalism. For my kickoff tune today, I went with REO Speedwagon's "Riding the Storm Out." We just made it, too. Zara Phillips jumped the last fence clear to win the Individual Gold, and the next thing you know, we were having a good old-fashioned frog strangler. Clayton Fredericks jumped a classy round to move up into the Silver slot, and how 'bout that Amy Tryon?

It was deja vu Athens all over again, where she comes into the ring in seventh place, jumps the money round, and this time gets the individual Bronze. Kim Severson gets all the press, but Kim would be the first to tell you that Amy is the rock we build the team on, and she did not let us down this time, we let her down. Despite Amy's medal, there are some long faces in the USET stables tonight. We need good horses and riders to back up the people we brought here, and right now we don't have them. Look at the Brits...there are not many other teams that could lose the Individual Gold medal winner, plus the winner of the Rolex Grand Slam, and still win the Silver...and they started two World Championship/Olympic rookies to do it. That is depth.

If I were a U.S. rider, age about 20, with a nice three-star horse, I would say to myself "Hmmmmm...the Olympics are in two years, the World Games will be here in Lexington in four years...I think I am going to go back out to the barn and ride with out stirrups for a while...'cause I want to ride for my country, and it looks like I have a chance." But it won't just happen. You have to make it happen. Good luck kid, you don't really realize how badly we need you and how much we are pulling for you. Now you run along to the stables and cross your stirrups while I tell the rest of these nice people about the rest of what I saw today.

I was thinking of trying to slip in some more of the stuff that got me in such trouble the other day, say, something like I have noticed that [*Watch it—your Net Nanny is on this site 24/7*].

OK. OK. It was worth a try. (Cue insane laughter sound track here.)

The course today was typically European. It was not quite as big, or as related, as the course at Rolex this spring, but it took a lot of jumping, and there were not many double clears. This is a big arena, and the jumping lines stretched from one end of the arena to the other. When you are on a slightly tired horse, that was whizzing around at 600 meters per minute yesterday, it is a tricky job to hold them together. If you fight with your horse, you knock rails down, but if you just let them run you knock rails down, so you have to find the right balance of control and aggression.

It also does not help that most riders are so nervous when they ride into a big time arena that they want to throw up. While I watched the jumping today, I got to thinking how rare Sunday afternoon nerve is. By this I mean it is rare to see people who can come in to an arena with their team and individual chances on the line, with a chance to go into the history books, and with a TV zoom lens showing every detail live to a worldwide audience, and then they ride better than you have ever seen them ride. That is Sunday afternoon nerve. Look up Sunday afternoon nerve in the dictionary, and you will see Amy Tryon's photo. She has got it. So does Clayton Fredericks, and Zara.

Of course, Zara is a special case. She has grown up with the tabloid press breathing down her neck, so that sort of thing doesn't bother her. But still, she didn't get into the ring because she is the Queen's grand daughter...she got in there because she rides her horse the living best. And when she gets in there, she makes the best of it...sounds simple, but a lot of people weren't able to do it today.

And talking about that zoom lens, when Zara went through the finish line, they had a close up shot of her face. She looked up at the main scoreboard, and confirmed in her own mind that she had just won the Gold medal. The she dropped her eyes to Toy Town, and gave him a little pat, and you could see her thinking, "You are so special, and I am so lucky to have the ride on you, and I really love you." In the meantime, Toy Town, who is a British sport horse, but looks and acts Irish, was googling his eyes at the crowd, and obviously going, "Eh, eh, did good, didn't I, Mom"

We were talking earlier about the type of horse that the short format would demand in the 21st century. Just for the record,

Toy Town is a British sport horse, Ben Along Time is an Irish sport horse, and Poggio is an American TB. Out of the next four? Two TB's and two warmbloods. And one of the TB's, Glengarrick, is 19 years old, and was unlucky not to jump a double clear...he barely touched the last rail in the triple. 19? That is like 120 in dog years.

We haven't talked much about the Germans winning the Gold team, basically because they won it fair and square, and beat everybody else's brains out. Did you see the margin of victory? 44 points? They could have knocked down 10 rails, and still won. Heck, even Kim didn't win Rolex by that much last year. Then the Brit's were ahead of the Aussies by 17 points. But the Aussies only beat us for the Bronze by less than a point. That is a gut-wrenching margin anywhere, and even worse at a competition of this magnitude. I can tell you from personal experience that all four of our riders will look at the ceiling in their motel room tonight, and go, "If only I had..." But we didn't, and the Germans did, and we have to suck it up and get better. That is all there is to it.

And this is about all there is to it, for me. I've really enjoyed my time here in Aachen, but am starting to get a little homesick. I've been married 40 years now, and my wife doesn't pay much attention to me any more. When we had our anniversary this year, somebody asked her if she had ever considered divorce. She replied, "Murder, yes. Divorce, never." Anyway, I'd better get back before she knows I am gone....I left a tape of me snoring, so she probably thinks I am still around the farm somewhere.

The NBC guys I have been working with, Bob Hughes, Jim Carr, and Bob Ives have been great to work with. They got involved with horse sports seven years ago, when they were hired to do Rolex. They started out looking at horses as just another TV job. And now? Let me tell you a little story about how they spent last night. I went to a party downtown and got back about 11. They were sitting in the living room, drinking local German beer, and watching the Kur finals live on Eurosport. Not only were they hooked on horses, but they were picking on the judges, whining about horses being irregular in the passage, and generally sounding like a bunch of died-in-the-wool horse fans. Cracked me up.

Naturally, I stayed and watched the rest of the rides with them. But I had to draw the line when they started watching "Triumph the Insult Comic Dog" from the *Late Night with Conan O'Brien*. [*Not true—This is Bob Hughes speaking—Executive Producer of the 2006 WEG, The 2008 Olympics, and the 2010 WEG from Lexington—Woff Laughed his...off*]

[*Bob. Oh, Bob. Not you too? Net Nannie is watching you...Behave or else.*]

Is there an echo in here? I must be overserved, or under-cocktailed, or something. I better go, I got a plane to catch, and grandkids to watch, and Labradors to check up on. I'll see you soon. In the meantime, good-bye from Aachen.

GALLOPING STILL

It is funny how some horses catch your eye. I wrote this article for the program at Rolex, when I heard that Prince Panache was going to be retired there. I had watched him grow up, and run at most of the big events of his generation, and I had loved him since I first saw him. He didn't always win, but he was a real gentleman, and he was always trying to do his best. That is a rare quality in man or beast.

He did not complete the World Games in Italy in 1998, because of a heart murmur. When he came back the following year, and was the high-point horse of the year in the U.S.A., I was the master of ceremonies for the awards banquet. "There is nothing wrong with this horse's heart," I said. I hope that after you read this, you will agree with me.

I always cry at retirement ceremonies. I don't expect that to change this Sunday, when we gather to watch Prince Panache take his final gallop around an arena that he competed in so many times over the past decade. As you watch him gallop by, you might take a moment to wonder, "What is it that makes a horse great?" Obviously, great horses are talented. They have more jumping power than the average horse, more speed, better balance, and fancier paces. Certainly they are durable. They bring an unquenchable love for the game, and a fierce competitive desire to every competition. They can surmount adversity and injury that would sideline normal athletes for the rest of their life. But still, there are a lot of horses in the fields surrounding the Kentucky Horse Park like that. You probably saw one as you drove here from the airport.

Is it that Prince Panache (Nache to his friends) was just lucky enough to have Karen O'Connor for a rider, and to be owned by Jacqueline Mars? Certainly, that is part of it. That pair has been one of the most successful owner-rider partnerships in the world over the past 10 years. But there must be something else, something more, which makes a horse special enough to make people come from all over the world, just to see him one more time, to pay their respects, before he steps out of the arena for the last time.

I have been watching these horses for more years than I would really like to remember right now, and I think I know what that quality is that we call great. That quality is heart. Heart is the intangible quality that makes a horse rise to the occasion, to walk flat-footed into a strange arena, thousands of miles from home, and get the best dressage score of his life. Or to keep going, no matter what the conditions, when any normal horse would throw in the towel. Heart makes a great horse successful where normal horses fail.

The factual details about Nash seem so dry and mundane:

Prince Panache
17 hand, dark bay thoroughbred gelding, by Nickel King
Foaled in 1984 at the Benyon's stud in Warwickshire, England.
Just another tall, gawky kid at the time.

A recitation of his record impresses you, but there are other equally successful horses around. Not many, but some. Won horse trials at every level, competed at the World Equestrian Games and Burghley, completed Badminton in fifth place, won the National Championships at Foxhall Farm, in Georgia, won here at the Kentucky Horse Park. Not bad for a big, gangly colt that couldn't get out of his own way. But sometimes a horse reveals himself not just when he wins an important competition, but when he transcends it. And so it was for me when I watched Nache at the Sydney Olympics in 2000.

Let me set the stage for you...it seemed to me in the spring of 2000 that the event world was coiling into a giant spring, preparing itself to fly halfway around the world to Sydney. The difficulties involved in sending teams that enormous distance seemed to call for extraordinary efforts from everyone. The riders, the horses, the coaches, the administrative staff, everyone. Efforts like that do not occur every year, and they make people nervous, and they generate pressure.

The pressure did not lessen when our squad got to Australia, as we speedily suffered the most incredible series of mishaps and accidents that any team has ever experienced. Yet when the final team was announced, I still thought we had the best chance for an Olympic medal that we had had in a long time. David O'Connor on Giltedge, Nina Fout on 3 Magic Beans, Linden Wiesman on Anderoo, and Karen O'Connor on Prince Panache were to ride in that order. Four lovely horses and riders with a nice mix of youth and experience.

I remember thinking, as I walked the cross-country course, that this was a true Olympic course. It had scope, it had complexity, and most of all, it was on very physical terrain. You have to understand that a four-mile cross-country course is one thing, but a four-mile cross-country course with a half-mile long uphill pull at the very end is a horse of a different color. If your horse was not fit, and tough, you were going to have to nurse him around, or you were going to be embarrassed in front of the whole world. I stopped when I got to the top of that hill, and looked back over the valley behind that ridge. From the valley floor, the course started a long, uphill, sinuous, climbing path to the top of the ridge and on to the finish line. "It will take a special kind of horse and rider to come storming up this hill," I thought. And indeed, it was to prove so.

"This horse is the ultimate professional," Karen O'Connor told me recently. "He seems to get calmer under pressure." If so, he was the only calm creature in the Olympic stadium at Horsley Park that hot afternoon. The various team's dressage scores were close, and while his three teammates had all performed personal bests, it was up to Nache to keep us in the hunt. So Nache sauntered into the arena, and proceeded to lower his previous best dressage score by an astounding 10 points. Just another day at the office.

On cross-country day, David was our lead off rider. He galloped a clear round, but a little steady, with a few time faults. This was gut wrenching, because the margin at this level is so small, and in a team competition you never know which of the three scores are going to count, or how the other teams are going to go. Even a few time faults might be enough to let another team in ahead of us.

Nina came next, on an obviously exuberant 3 Magic Beans. By dint of much struggling, Nina jumped a clear round, but Beans was a runaway, and Nina wisely saved a clear round by sacrificing time. Two good rounds on the board. Two more horses to go and we only needed one more good round, to have a chance at a medal.

Then it was Linden's turn. She set out well, but a lost shoe and slippery going defeated Anderoo, and Linden pulled him up, and patted his neck, and looked off into the shimmering heat of a long Australian afternoon for an instant, and watched her dreams evaporate like a mirage.

Now it was all down to Karen and Nache, who set out like they did this sort of thing every day.

"This is the bravest cross-country horse I have ever ridden," Karen said later. I thought that too, as I watched him during the early part of the course, but what really struck me at that moment was the uncanny intelligence Nache brought to every situation. By the time he jumped, you had the feeling that he had walked each fence beforehand.

"With Nache," said Karen, "I really had the feeling at the beginning of his career that I was the one helping him to become famous. But by the Olympics, Nache had taken over, and now I was the one in the shadows, and he was the one in the spotlight."

And the spotlight was truly on him now, because all the hopes of the U.S. contingent were based on him jumping a clean, and fast, round.

"Clear through the first water," the announcer reported, followed by, "Clear through the second water." Then a heart stopping, "A bit of a scramble at the sunken road...but they're all right, and going well at the three-quarter mark." Then a hush fell over the course, as the announcement came. "Karen O'Connor and Prince Panache have been held on course. The course has been put on an indefinite hold."

Being held on course is a nightmare for a rider, because they can't tell how much time they have left to get home. The officials stop the time before they notify the rider, so the rider doesn't know how long their time has been held, or how long the hold will be. As if that were not difficult enough, the only thing Karen knew for sure was that she could not afford any time faults, if she were to keep her team in the running.

So there they were, at the bottom of a long, heartbreaking hill, with 10 Olympic fences to go, and no idea what pace would be needed, no idea what the scores for the other teams were, only the cold, hard fact that now it was all or nothing. What a weight was on their shoulders, as they walked quietly in circles, waiting for the signal to restart. Not just the weight of their own chances, but of their teammate's as well, who were waiting at the finish line. The endless hours of practice, the time away from home, the inevitable disappointments along the way, the incredible expenditure of time and effort and money, all to chase a dream, a dream of being the best. All of it had come down to this moment. And there they were, on "indefinite hold."

Karen and Nache could have been forgiven for looking up that long, long slope, and thinking, "No. No, we can't do it. It's not fair; it's too much to ask. We have broken our rhythm, and we won't be able to get it back. We have come a long way, and jumped a lot of jumps. After all we have given over the years, and all we have done today, to ask us to give anything more here, it's not right. It's not fair. We won't do it. We can't do it." But we know now, that's not what happened.

At this point, those of us who were there were in an agony of suspense. We knew Karen and Nache were clear to that point, we knew they were held on course, and we knew they could manage to get home somehow. But the team needed a clean round, and not just clean, but fast. There were no more U.S. riders, no one else we could turn to. It was up to Karen and Nache, and it was now or never.

I was a spotter at the first water complex, so I could not see into the valley where they were waiting. I could see the last two fences at the top of the ridge, and the finish line. All I could do was wait, seething with impatience and sick with the frustration of those who can do nothing to affect the outcome.

Then I heard a roar from the crowd, and knew they were on their way. By now, it was late in the afternoon. The shadows were growing longer and darker in the valley, but the ridge was still sun-lit, and a haze of dust lent a glow to the scene. And then they came into view, and I suddenly knew that it was going to be all right.

Since then, I have watched the tapes over and over, and I still think that it is the bravest performance I have ever seen. There is a moment, after Karen and Nache have restarted, after they have jumped a fence, and reestablished their rhythm, when Karen bends over, and asks Nache if he can do it. Can he race up that last long, steep, drawn-out run to the finish line, and more importantly, can he do it at a racing pace? There is no way to know how much time is left. The only thing to do is to gallop as fast as mortal flesh and blood can gallop, and to jump at a pace that normal horse and rider would never consider. Never mind fatigue, never mind fear. We have to go. Now.

All this, and more, Karen whispered in Nache's ear, and he answered, as God answered Joshua, "I will not fail thee nor forsake thee."

So they galloped up into view, into a golden glow, into the history books, and into our hearts. And I thought at that moment that I had been given an insight into one of the most remarkable horses I have ever seen.

Prince Panache is retired now, but if you look to the west, when the shadows are long, and the sun casts a golden glow upon the land, you will see him, galloping still.

FINDING CARAWICH

When it comes to horses, I think of myself as a fairly mechanical trainer. Squeeze your hands and the horse will slow down, close your legs and your horse will speed up...that sort of thing. However, there is more to it than that. Spend any amount of time around horses, and you will become convinced that there is a communication between horses and humans that can't be measured. The worst among them sense our fears, and take advantage of us: and the best among them sense our dreams, and take us where we have always longed to go. For example, take Carawich...

Not many people get a chance to ride in the Olympics. During the time that you are involved in the training and selection process, you don't have time to think about anything else. If the stars align for you, then you are too busy riding at the Olympics to think about it. It is only after the Games are over that you get a chance to think about your experiences, to wonder about the long, hard, winding path that brought you there, and especially about how incredibly lucky you were to have a horse good enough to ride in the Olympics. And you can't help wondering if you will ever find such a horse again.

By the spring of 1977, I had ridden in the Olympics twice, but that experience was receding into the past. I had not been on a team of any sort for five years, and indeed had not won any competition above the preliminary level since 1972. I had endured an endless succession of horses that were almost good enough, but when you ride at that level, "almost" won't do. I had not given up on my dreams yet, but I was beginning to wonder if one day soon I might have to exchange dreams for reality.

I was coaching at Badminton that spring, and was standing in the courtyard of the Duke of Badminton's hunter stables, waiting for the first veterinary examination to start. Lars Sederholm came up to me, and we stood there talking for a moment. Lars is a genius horseman who had a terrific influence on my riding, so I always enjoy a chance to catch up with him. By now the horses had started to walk around the outside of the courtyard, and we moved up to the crowd control barrier to watch the proceedings. Lars was distracted by someone, so I stood at the barrier alone for a moment, and watched all these wonderful creatures walk past.

I suddenly noticed a big, handsome, mealy-nosed, dark brown horse walking towards me. He had an enormous, smooth, flowing walk, and he caught my eye immediately. Just as he got next to me, he stopped, and turned his head towards me. I had the sudden, eerie feeling that he was looking directly into my eyes, and that I had been picked out, and was being evaluated. I stood, spellbound, while the hair literally stood up on the back of my neck. I can't say how long he stood like that, looking at me, because time had stopped for me, and I was not aware of crowd noise or other people around me, or anything but this horse, staring intently into my eyes.

The horses' groom tugged impatiently on his lead shank, yet he stood a moment longer, looking at me. Then he seemed to say "hmmm" to himself, turned his head forward, and walked on with that powerful, athletic walk.

I grabbed Lars by the arm, interrupted his conversation, and asked him, "Who is *that*?" pointing at the horse's receding form.

"Oh, that's Carawich," Lars replied, "he is a wonderful horse, but you'll never buy him."

I said "OK" to Lars, but I was thinking, "What a strange experience I've just had." I watched Carawich go for the rest of the weekend, and he was indeed wonderful. But when I returned to the U.S.A., I put the whole experience out of my mind.

International rules in those days required that the rider and the owner of horse be of the same nationality by January 1 of the year of the World Championships or Olympics, to be eligible to compete. By now it was early December of 1977, and I was starting to realize that I probably was not going to get a chance to ride in the 1978 World Championships. All the good U.S. horses were already taken, and my search for horses in other countries had come up empty. I was 34 years old, fit, and at whatever peak of my abilities I was going to achieve. If I did not ride in the World Championships, it would be a long, dark three-year period of training, with not much hope that I might make the team for the Olympics in 1980. It made me sad, but that was just the way it was, and I might as well get used to it.

During that period of my life, I did some buying and selling of English and Irish horses. I had been looking for a horse for a client, and suddenly thought I might give Lars Sederholm a call, to see if he had anything for sale.

"Hello, Jimmie," Lars said, "What a coincidence. I have just now hung up with Carawich's owner. His rider is pregnant, and they have decided to put Carawich on the market."

"Well, call them back and tell them he is sold pending a vet exam," I said. We chatted for another few minutes about other horses, and then I hung up the phone. "Now what," I thought. I did not have the money to pay for Carawich, so I wound up borrowing against my life insurance policy. It was the best business move I have ever made.

We got the deal done in time to have my name on the ownership papers before the first of the year, and I started a partnership with the best horse I would ever ride. I can remember to this instant that when I slid onto his back for the first time, I felt as if I were putting on a glove. I rode him for four years, and there was never a time when I did not feel that he could read my mind. If I tacked him up for some dressage work, he stood like a statue. But when I put his jumping saddle on, he would start to dance and fly kick in the cross ties...he knew the difference before I could even get on him.

When he arrived, he had a horrible, demeaning stable name. I put a lot of store by a horse's stable name, but I am also very superstitious, and it is supposed to be bad luck to change a horse's stable name; "Well, my friend," I thought, "you are getting a new lease on life, and my riding life has definitely taken a turn for the better, so I am going to change your stable name and call you "Pop." You have a hell of a pop over a jump, and Pop is what the cowboys call the wisest and most experienced cowboy."

Pop gave me my greatest thrill on horseback at the Alternate Olympics in 1980. Basically, he sensed the importance of the occasion, and ran away with me around a formidable cross-country course. This is not the approved strategy for the first rider in a team, but I had no real choice in the matter. Pop had taken over. The only thing I can say for myself is that I had enough sense to sit quietly and let him run his race. We finished with the fastest round of the day, and an Individual Silver medal. Is it any wonder that I loved him above all horses?

Let me tell you one more story before I close this section: Horsemen don't let horses rub their face on them. It is considered rude, and you have to be careful about letting an animal that outweighs you by 1,000 pounds push you around. After I had been with Pop for a while, I decided that I would suspend that rule for him. He appreciated this, and would greet me every morning with the most ferocious face rub. When he retired, I put him in the south field here at our farm in Upperville, VA, with Alex.

From time to time, I see horses that I instinctively like, and know how to ride. I had seen Alex as a four-year-old, but it would be 10 years before the USET let me ride him. Of course, when I did, we won the National Championships, but that is another story. Anyway, no matter how fond I was of Alex, he did not rub his face on me. He knew the rules, and respected the bond between Pop and me. When I would go to the south field to check on them, they would walk up to me at the gate, and Pop would luxuriate in a long and thorough face rub on me, at the expense of my shirt and sweater.

After I had to put Pop to sleep, I could not go down to the south field for a couple of days, as I knew it would be too painful. But I had to go down, to see how Alex was doing on his own. When I called him, he marched right up to me, and rubbed his face on my chest. I was crying as he did it, and I think Alex was, too.

PART III

VERSE

THE MIDLAND-PIEDMONT FOX HOUND TRIAL

I wrote this poem for the final dinner celebrating the Midland-Piedmont Foxhound Trial. The dinner was held at St. Brides, which is one of the loveliest estates one could ever imagine. I tried to make an historical record of the Trials, which accounts for the references to the various farms and estates here in the Piedmont country. Local legend has it that there is a fox with two brushes that haunts the countryside. He has been pursued from time immemorial, but George Washington never caught him, and modern day sportsmen have likewise failed. You only spy the two-brushed fox on a full moon, and only then if you believe in him. I freely admit to sighting him on more than one occasion, but then I have always maintained that scotch improves my vision.

In this poem, he also serves as the conscience of the sporting community, and warns us of the importance of the countryside to all our pursuits. If we don't care for it, we will lose it. If we look after it, we will be blessed with many more contests held in the countryside, contests where the countryside is the true winner.

DECEMBER 5-12, 1991

The Piedmont Fox stretched, and licked his chops, and flicked his two-brushed tail.

He trotted through Atoka Farm and perched against a rail.

He felt no fear, the moon was sere, and dying in the west.

You cannot see the Piedmont Fox until the moon is full,

And only then if you believe, believe with all your will.

The sportsman born may seldom glimpse this ghostly apparition, city dwellers never.

Those who've seen will rarely say how they came to view him, for it's their secret ever.

Some sudden intuition makes them turn and meet his gaze

And hold it for a moment, then watch in silent awe

The Piedmont Fox vanish in the haze.

He reappeared at Hastening to watch the Midland Pack.

He walked into the Furr Road side, and perched upon a stack.

He'd seen the Midland Hounds before; he knew their drive and pluck.

"If Piedmont's going to best this bunch," he thought, "they'll need a bit of luck."

And Midland drove their fox that day, drove him straight and true.

'Til all three judges pulled their faces and muttered, "What to do? What to do?"

For now the clash was truly joined—these titans of the chase

Would give no quarter, man or beast, and each would have their innings.

The Piedmont Fox turned and sauntered west, and thought,

"Good beginnings. Good beginnings."

Saturday broke fair and clear, and much too warm for scent.

But Piedmont's hounds did their best, brave and true and diligent.

So Sunday came and all retired to lick their wounds and rest,

And none could say at this, halfway, which of the packs was best.

The Piedmont Fox jumped the creek at Miller's Farm, and trotted up the hill.

Monday's meet was half past nine, he knew they'd be there still.

Bear's Den field was huge, so great a stir had this contest started.

And Midland quickly jumped two fox, and just as quickly chose the best

And waited not for horn or voice, but headed for the west.

Full hour's flight, a glorious sight of lovely pandemonium.

Atop Sky Hill they gave it best, and staggered home to take their rest.

Now the country round began to buzz, in endless speculation.

Yet none was brave enough to say this classic trials summation.

As Tuesday dawned, the two-brushed Fox cantered past Fox Covert,

He turned due east, into Foxlease, to see what Piedmont had to offer.

He wisely watched, perched near The Hut, and heard the coverts ring.

For Piedmont found their fox that day, and made the country sing.

And made the country sing.

Now Midland's chance was Wednesday's meet, and Welbourne greeted fair.

The Piedmont Fox tipped his nose to Moseby's Ghost, and vanished in the air.

And Midland had a day, indeed, a day to end all days.

All now remarked as how the judge's hair was turning grey, turning grey.

Thursday came and both packs knew this was their final chance.

St. Brides sat in the center, the jewel of all our land.

And both packs dove into the woods, to find a fox at hand.

They hunted south, they hunted west, they found the scent was nil.

They crossed Goose Creek and Milan Mill, and trotted up to Oak Spring Hill.And as they vanished in the mist, none would choose between them.

The Piedmont Fox aimed for Rokeby, tired but content.

"I think I have the answer near," he thought, "I think I see it clear.

No one's to be the victor here, and never any loser.

The countryside takes the prize; I'm sure by my last breath.

But all who took part here shall ever be the best."

Then the Piedmont Fox flicked both his brushes, and ambled off to rest.

SAGE DESAPERICIDO 1981

Labrador retrievers have been a part of my entire life. I am like a man without a shadow when I don't have at least one black Lab trotting at my heels. Most of them have been firmly of the opinion that somewhere there is a village with a missing idiot. Until that village comes and reclaims me, my Labs view it as their job to keep a close eye on me, as there is no telling what I will get up to next.

Thus I tend to get terribly fond of them, and suffer when I lose one. The death of a much-loved pet is wrenching enough, but it is far worse when a young dog disappears, never to return. Sage went out for a walk one morning, and never came home again. The title of the poem is from the South American terrorist's practice of desapericido, or "disappearing," people whose families they wish to terrorize. I'll never know what happened, but I will always wonder about Sage, and worry.

I suppose some truck stopped
On a quiet dirt road,
Some stranger spoke
A quiet word,
And Sage jumped in,
A long time ago.
But I miss him still.
I see him so clearly;
I always will.
I had gone to buy a Labrador
And found a friend instead.
He chose me—it sometimes happens,
He left his litter mates
To come and sit against my ankle
And survey his world with a
Somber, level, direct gaze.
He had not grown into his skin,
It fell in folds over his eyes
And hid his thoughts.
I never knew 'til later
That he had vowed
To serve me all his days.
I gathered him
All black fur and puppy breath,
Close to my heart, and lifted
Him into my life, and out the door.
Had I known what was in store,
He would have weighed far more.
At the end of each day,
He only asked—he thought it fair—
To collapse at my feet by my green leather chair,
With an audible "oof," and a grumbling sigh,
I, content to have him by,
He, content to remain there.
I never thought to ask him
Why, or how he would go
Or to tell him I
Would miss him so.

When they leave unexplained,
There's a tear in your heart.
Life's tapestry seems pulled apart.
Was there a reason? Was it ordained?
Why did it have to be this way,
That he would go, and I would stay?
He would be dead by now
If he had stayed, buried
With a small stone at his head.
But he's disappeared, so he's buried
In my heart instead.
I miss him still;
I loved him so;
I wish I'd told him, just once more,
Before he had to go.

THE FOALS
AT
SNOW HILL

Looking back at some of the previous chapters, they seem a little sad to me, so I thought I would end this book with a poem about hope, and about the future. A few years ago, Gail and I were in Maryland, visiting with "Duck" and Glennie Martin. The Martins own the farm where the Maryland Hunt Cup is run every year, hence the reference to the third fence in the poem. Glennie asked us to take a drive over to their farm at Snow Hill, to look at some weanling thoroughbreds. Another house guest, Daphne Wood, came along, and as we walked down the stable aisle, looking at the foals, I heard Glennie and Daphne commenting on the markings on the foals. "Look," said Daphne, "a star, and a snip, like a Christmas tree."

For some reason that line stayed in my mind, and the next thing I knew I had written a poem about the foals at Snow Hill. Young animals, and young children, give us the greatest gift that anyone can receive. They give us joy, and hope for the future.

A Star and a Snip, a Christmas Tree,
What will these markings mean to me
in the years to be?
Will he gallop and run,
Will she jump for fun,
Or, just lie in the sun?
What stage will they stand on,
What games will they play,
Will they make me cry on some special day?
A bay at the third, a grey on the line,
Some famous finish, frozen in time,
Or a lady's hack, quiet and fine
Will he gallop till dark, a hunter's thrill
Will she show us famous courage and will,
Or leave holes in our hearts time cannot fill.
I dream of their talent, hope for the best,
Train them to be equal to any test,
Pray they will be faster than all the rest.
A star and a snip, a Christmas tree,
What will these markings mean to me
in the years to be?
I wonder,
I wonder,
I can't wait to see!